Observer's Directory of
Royal Naval Submarines
1901–1982

Observer's Directory of
Royal Naval Submarines
1901–1982

M. P. Cocker

with drawings by
John Lambert

Foreword by
Vice Admiral Sir Lancelot Bell Davies, KBE

This book is published and distributed
in the United States by the
UNITED STATES NAVAL INSTITUTE
Annapolis, Maryland 21402

By the same author
Destroyers of the Royal Navy, 1893–1981

Frontispiece
Orpheus on exercise in Rothesay Bay.

First published by Frederick Warne (Publishers) Ltd London, 1982

ISBN 0 7232 2964 3

Filmset and printed by
BAS Printers Limited, Over Wallop, Hampshire

CONTENTS

ACKNOWLEDGEMENTS

I am deeply indebted to the following individuals and/or Institutions, for help and advice during the compilation of this book. Additionally, I am grateful for permission to use their drawings and photographs.
In random order they are:
W. K. Fox, Cammell Laird Shipbuilders, Mrs R. M. Wayman, Michell Bearings; Cdr F. E. R. Phillips, RN and Cdr F. N. Ponsonby MVO, RN, Public Relations Office, MOD (N); Lt Cdr M. R. Wilson, Naval Historical Branch MOD (N); D. W. Robinson and W. G. Clouter, Vickers Shipbuilding and Engineering Ltd.; G. Britton, Royal Navy Submarine Museum; J. Anderson, Scotts Shipbuilding Company Limited; G. B. Vaughton and D. Thornley, Manchester Ship Canal Company; Mrs G. Wilkinson, Nashua Copycat; Mrs T. Crook, Marconi Space Defence Systems Limited; M. Willis, Imperial War Museum.

My wife Pauline has been particulary helpful in typing the manuscript and E. F. Bunt has been of great assistance in research. If by any chance I have omitted any individual or organization, I trust that my apology will be accepted and understood.

The general arrangement drawings have all been specially prepared by John Lambert.

Permission to reproduce the photographs is gratefully acknowledged, in particular to Vickers Shipbuilding Ltd, from whose archives all have been supplied except those noted below. Thanks are also due to Scotts Shipbuilding Ltd: pages 30, 31, 41, 46; Cammell Laird Ltd: 62, 67, 94, 98, 100; Imperial War Museum: 67, 80; Ufficio Storico Marina Militare Italiana: 84, 85; Ministry of Defence (Navy): 2, 8, 10, 100, 101, 104, 105, 107, 109, 110, 111, 113, 114, 115, 121; Marconi Space and Defence Systems Ltd: 122, 123; Royal Naval Submarine Museum: 19, 33, 53, 59, 83, 89, 91, 92, 93; Scott Lithgow Ltd: 40; G. Carter: 76; Fleet Air Arm Museum: 120.

FOREWORD
by
Vice Admiral Sir Lancelot Bell Davies, KBE

The *Observer's Directory of Royal Naval Submarines* is published at the very moment that naval history has recorded a further significant change in naval warfare. The Falklands campaign will occupy historians for years to come. It contains many 'firsts' and many lessons. Single-ship successful actions always sparkle in the pages of history; but few mark a major turning point in naval warfare.

The sinking of the Argentine cruiser *General Belgrano* by HM S/M *Conqueror* marked such a turning point. It is the first time that a major surface combatant has been sunk by a dived submarine, capable of keeping up with its target indefinitely, and able to select the tactical moment to strike, under the operational command of a headquarters 8,000 miles away.

The immediate effect was to deny the Argentine suface naval forces any further participation in the conflict. Few single-ship actions have had such a profound strategic result.

The full story of the Royal Naval submarines' contribution to that conflict will rightly remain undisclosed for some time to come; but the impact of their presence upon the imagination of their foes goes without saying.

Imagination is also the spur of the student. Any serious researcher will welcome this directory, because it provides a convenient and comprehensive catalogue of British submarines from which he can check statistical data.

But it does more than this. Anyone whose imagination is inspired by warships probably finds that browsing through an old illustrated naval reference book is a very satisfying pastime. The older the copy the better. There is something magical about the photograph of an old warship that stimulates the storyteller in us all. It matters not that the picture is a formal one, nor that the statistics are ungarnished by historical narrative—imagination thrives best without such interference.

The snag with such an old book is that it freezes time in the year of its issue. In this new directory Mr Cocker gives us the luxury of daydreaming through time as well as checking up on facts.

The advent of nuclear propulsion has provided a dramatic change to capability, and a marked improvement in the submariner's lifestyle; but the make-up of the man is the same. His courage, forebearance and tolerance of his shipmates, and his dedicated professionalism, will continue to provide food for the historian, and inspiration for the imagination of those who dream of the sea.

Thank you Mr Cocker for providing such an invaluable help to both.

Oracle preparing to enter harbour, her ship's crest and bell already in position on the conning tower. The flare of the bow is very noticeable at this angle.

INTRODUCTION

The purpose of this book is to fill an important gap in naval history. There has not previously been a book recording every submarine commissioned into the Royal Navy: this is an attempt to provide an illustrated directory to each one and also show the evolution of the submarine since 1901.

There are obvious difficulties in compiling a record of this type: the service histories of many of the boats (submarines are traditionally still called boats) could each fill a book. It is left to others to describe such exploits. Similarly, there are continual modifications to the design of all but the smallest Classes. While such minutiae are of interest to the specialist, they are limited here, for the sake of brevity and clarity, to the more important changes.

From the Holland Class of 1901 to the Type 2400, announced in 1979, the wheel has come full circle: the earliest submarines were powered by internal combustion engines and electric motors. Now, having gone through a cycle which has included steam turbines, both oil- and nuclear-driven, the latest designs are again planned to be diesel-powered as were the earlier ones.

The first boats were armed with just one torpedo tube. Soon their number multiplied; guns worthy of a battleship were fitted; aircraft were carried; the submarine cruiser has armament equal to that of a frigate—though only for surface action. Today the torpedo remains the standard weapon and the heavy gun has been succeeded by the sub-surface to air and sub-surface to surface missiles. Another thing has changed—submariners have always needed stamina, but now more than ever with submarines which can, it is said, stay submerged for a year.

M. P. Cocker

New Moston
Manchester

Repulse in the Gare Loch. The 'parrot's beak' on the fore casing contains a Sonar system.

A BRIEF ACCOUNT OF THE SUBMARINE IN THE ROYAL NAVY

In the closing years of the nineteenth century only France could claim near-parity in sea power with Great Britain. The 'Entente Cordiale' was a decade away and France was regarded as a potential naval threat. This hazard increased by successful French attempts to build 'sousmarins'. Four such vessels were in use in the French navy by 1897, electrically powered and with compressed air reservoirs; the largest was 160 ft long and displaced 266 tons.

It was not that the British were ignorant of submarine development. In 1866 Vickers had built a submarine designed by Nordenfelt, a Swedish gun-maker, for the Russian navy, but she was wrecked on her maiden voyage to St Petersburg. These craft depended on vertically mounted propellers in conjunction with ballast tanks to make them submerge. They were powered by steam engines[1] on the surface which, as was found later in the British 'K' Class, created a number of problems, including the fact that they took longer to be ready to dive than boats driven by other means.

The British Admiralty believed that its surface fleet was more than a sufficient match for such outlandish vessels and it was not considered necessary for the Royal Navy to be interested in them, though no doubt British Intelligence kept an eye on French progress.

The British attitude changed because the self-propelled torpedo provided a practical submarine weapon. In 1866 Robert Whitehead had invented this 'devil's device' which travelled beneath the water driven by compressed air. It maintained a constant depth by means of a hydrostatic valve and horizontal rudders, and Whitehead later added a servo motor and gyroscope for directional stability. The British government acquired rights to it in 1871.

In 1877 J. P. Holland, an Irish-born American immigrant,[2] applied the horizontal rudder to the submarine boats he was developing and his design was taken up by the Admiralty who placed the contract with Vickers for five Holland boats in 1900. It was the beginning of an association which has extended to the Type 2400, announced in 1979 for building in the 1980s.

Thus it was that the 'submarine' first appeared in the Royal Navy in 1901. The first Holland boat was $63\frac{3}{4} \times 11\frac{3}{4} \times 10$ ft draught on the surface; it displaced 104 tons on the surface and 122 tons submerged. It had a single 14 in torpedo tube in the bow and a surface speed of eight knots (five knots submerged). By comparison, the Holland VIII, built in the same year for the United States Navy, displaced 76 tons, but had the same surface speed.

Vickers' design staff developed changes to the Holland design and produced the Class A design which was built under the superintendence of the Admiralty. The 13 boats of this Class were followed by 11 boats in Class B in 1906 and 38 in the C Class which were completed by 1910. Displacement had now reached 290 tons on the surface and 320 tons submerged, and the armament increased to two 18 in tubes. A 16 cyl petrol engine provided surface power and charged the batteries for the electric motor for use when submerged. D and E Classes followed, the first Classes to depart from a purely coastal concept, and were the last to be completed before World War I. D Class had bow and stern torpedo tubes. E Class was the first also to have beam tubes

[1] These early steam engines relied upon the latent heat principle and so were different from the steam turbines used in the *Swordfish* and K Classes.
[2] J. P. Holland (1840–1914) first became involved in submarine design with a view to their use against the British in the Irish fight for independence. After emigrating to America he had mixed fortune in designing boats for the US Navy and also worked for Russia and Japan.

C22 on trials.

and the first to include boats converted for minelaying. The first submarine to be mounted with a deck gun was *D4*, on which was fitted a single 12 pdr.

Of the World War I Classes, the small and not very successful F Class was followed by the V Class of four boats; G Class of 14 boats were the first to be fitted with a 21 in stern tube in addition to four 18 in tubes at the bow.

These relatively small patrol submarines were limited in their range and there was an urgent need for boats which would be capable of working with the Fleet. The first venture to this end was the *Nautilus*, built by Vickers in 1914. She was $242\frac{1}{2}$ ft long and displaced 1,270 tons surfaced. Her power plant of diesel and electric motors gave her a surface speed of 17 knots (10 knots submerged). Although commissioned, she was not a success and never became operational. The experiments continued on a different tack with *Swordfish*, launched in 1916, which was powered by a steam turbine on the surface and by twin electric motors when submerged. She too suffered numerous problems and was finally converted to be a surface patrol vessel at Portsmouth in 1917. The steam turbine theme was continued in the K Class, of which 18 were built. They were the fastest submarines afloat for many years, and not beaten on the surface until *Dreadnought* in 1963. They achieved a surface speed of 24 knots from twin steam turbines and also had a diesel auxiliary engine, plus twin electric motors for submerged running. A somewhat miscellaneous armament included a 3 in gun or two 4 in guns, machine guns and a depth charge thrower. Although designed to work with the Fleet on the surface as a scout vessel, possibly in weather too severe for a destroyer, there were many accidents culminating in two collisions in January 1918. Many of the crews were lost and the Class was phased out of service in the 1920s.

At the insistence of Commodore(S) S. S. Hall the M Class was embarked upon following the development of the German U-cruiser. Three boats were completed, each with a 12 in gun. This was replaced on one with a seaplane; the other was converted for minelaying.

Other Classes of more conventional design included the H and J Classes, H Class in particular being most successful on operations, and 37 were built. The last Class of World War I was given the letter R, with ten boats. Though conventional in design they were noteworthy for being nearly twice as fast submerged (15 knots) as they were on the surface ($9\frac{1}{2}$ knots).

After World War I the victorious powers met to reach agreement on the size of their post-war fleets. Great Britain and the USA were in favour of the abolition of submarines, but were opposed by France and Japan; Italy had reservations. It was agreed that none of the contracting powers would possess more than three boats larger than 2,000 tons displacement and that no submarine would carry a gun larger than 8 in calibre. The total submarine tonnage permitted was 52,700 tons for any one of the contracting powers. Great Britain, Japan and the USA agreed to the figures.

X1, launched in 1923, was another 'one boat' experimental Class described as a 'cruiser submarine' as she carried four 5.2 in guns in two turrets in addition to six 21 in torpedo tubes.

The new construction programme in between the world wars produced the O, P and R Classes of 1,475 tons, 1,760 tons and 1,740 tons, respectively, on the surface. They were armed with a 4 in gun on a built up fore deck forward of the conning tower which enabled the ammunition to be passed up more easily and speedily. The gun was also at a higher level than before which made sighting easier and in heavy seas the crew did not have to leave the conning tower to use the gun.

There followed a design of three boats known as the Thames Class. The intention was that these should follow up the ill-fated K Class by being Fleet submarines. They displaced 2,185 tons surfaced and had a top speed of ten knots submerged. The complement of 61 was large for its time (although *X1* had a planned complement of 110) and were reported to be most comfortable.

In 1931 launching of the S Class commenced with four boats of low tonnage (735 tons surfaced), built for short sea operations, with a range of 3,750 nm. The Class design was good and a second group of eight were built with a slightly larger displacement of 765 tons. As World War II neared, the third S Class group was commenced and the Class was still being launched in 1945. It reached a total of 50 boats.

The first of the Porpoise Class of six boats designed as minelayers, was launched in 1932. They carried 50 mines and were also armed with six 21 in torpedo tubes in the bow and a 4 in deck gun.

They were followed by the U and V Classes, originally conceived as unarmed training boats and re-designed for their armament of four 21 in torpedo tubes, supplemented by a 3 in gun mounted forward of the conning tower. But there was no hatch giving direct access to the gun (probably because the Class had not been designed to carry one), with the result that the conning tower became overcrowded during a gun action.

The T Class, built from 1937 to 1945 in three groups of 15, 7 and 31 boats, were of much larger tonnage (1,325 tons, surfaced). They provided a very steady gun platform and a variety of torpedo tube positions. The first group had six internal and two external bow tubes, and there were a further two external tubes amidships, facing forward. Later construction also included an external stern tube and the midship tubes were reversed to fire aft.

During World War II the Royal Navy was also loaned boats from the US Navy R and S Classes, vintage

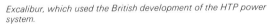
Excalibur, which used the British development of the HTP power system.

1914–1918; one German U-boat was captured off Iceland and was commissioned into the Royal Navy as HMS *Graph*. Two or three Italian boats were temporarily commissioned and the Royal Navy took over, again temporarily, four boats which were being built in the UK for the Turkish Navy.

Mention must also be made of the X craft midget submarines which had many successes in attacks on heavily defended enemy harbours.

The first of the post-World War II Classes was commenced in 1943. This was the new A Class of 15 boats which continued to be built until 1948. A conversion from the original design enabled them to be fitted with the Snorkel breathing equipment, allowing fresh air to be fed to the main engines when all but the snort tubes and periscopes were submerged. These boats displaced 1,385 tons surfaced and had a submerged speed no greater than eight knots. Numbers of the A and T Classes were modernised and 'streamlined' by removal of the deck gun. Apart from those used in the Indonesian confrontation, deck armament was no longer standard equipment. They were the last of over 40 years of design with 'conventional' power systems.

The Oberon and Porpoise Classes, of 13 and 8 boats, respectively, were completed from 1958 and were an intermediate stage before the first of the nuclear-powered submarines, *Dreadnought*, which was completed in 1963. With a surface displacement of 3,500 tons, she is powered by an S5W nuclear reactor through a geared steam turbine to a single propeller. The reversion to a single screw applies to all subsequent nuclear-powered boats.

The building programme of hunter-killer nuclear-powered submarines began with the Valiant Class completed in 1966; it was followed by the Churchill Class (1970), Swiftsure Class (1974) and the Trafalgar launched in 1981, nameship of her Class.

The Type 2400, the successor to the Oberon Class, returns to the traditional diesel power and is to a design jointly conceived by Vickers Shipbuilding and the Ministry of Defence (Navy).

In 1914, 61 boats were shown in commission. By 1918 the number had increased to 141, and at the close of World War II, 131 submarines were in commission (excluding boats captured from the enemy and being evaluated). By 1960 the figure had fallen to 53; in 1981, 30 submarines were either in commission or undergoing extensive refit.

NOTES AND ABBREVIATIONS

All names and numbers of boats and ships are Royal Navy designations, except where specifically stated otherwise. 'HMS' and 'HM S/M' have been omitted to avoid tedious repetition, except where necessary for clarity.

Commonwealth and Allied submarines are not included, except in a few specific instances when some part of their service was with the Royal Navy.

Dimensions, tonnages and units of power are expressed in 'imperial' units—i.e. ft, tons and hp. The conversion factors for metrication are:

from feet to metres: × 0.3048
from tons to tonnes: × 1.106

A Class defines a basic design of boat. Most Classes, however, underwent modification to greater or lesser extent. Only alterations of major significance are noted.

The complement is the number of Naval personnel planned to crew the vessel.

Shaft (i.e. propeller shaft): the number of these almost invariably accords with the number of engines or motors. Mention of the number of shafts is therefore only noted when there is a variation from the norm or if the text is unclear.

In illustrating many of the early submarines—and as recently as those in service in World War II—recourse has frequently had to be made to archival material. Many of the photographs show signs of their age, have been copied from earlier work, or were never of the highest rank. They are included because of their intrinsic historic interest.

The following abbreviations have been employed throughout the book:

AA	anti-aircraft
A/S	anti-submarine
bp	between perpendiculars
bhp	brake horsepower
DP	dual purpose
E-boat	high speed German patrol boat
HA	high angle
HE	high explosive
LA	low angle
MA/SB	motor anti-submarine boat
mg	machine gun
M/S	minesweeper
MTB	motor torpedo boat
mtg	mounting (for gun)
MV	motor vessel
nm	nautical mile
pdr	pounder (weight of gun projectile)
shp	shaft horsepower
SS	steam ship
TB	torpedo boat (Italian)
tubes	torpedo tubes
wl	waterline (length)
WT	wireless telegraph

Complete key to details identified on the General Arrangement Drawings

1 TRIMMING TANK
2 STEERING GEAR COMPARTMENT
3 MAIN ENGINE ROOM
4 MAIN ENGINE
5 MAIN MOTOR
6 FEED WATER
7 TURBINE ROOM
8 BATTERY SPACE
9 CONTROL ROOM
10 CREW ACCOMMODATION
11 WARD ROOM
12 AFTER TORPEDO TUBES
13 AFTER TORPEDO STOWAGE
14 BEAM TORPEDO TUBES
15 FORWARD TORPEDO TUBES
16 FORWARD TORPEDO STOWAGE
17 FUEL TANKS (DIESEL OR PETROL)
18 REACTOR ROOM
19 RADIO ROOM
20 MAIN BALLAST TANK
21 DIESEL ROOM
22 BOILER ROOM
23 'Q' TANK
24 'SNORT' MAST
25 SEARCH PERISCOPE
26 ATTACK PERISCOPE
27 W/T MAST
28 RADAR MAST
29 4 in GUN
30 3 in GUN
31 SONAR ROOM

Note: Each drawing is accompanied by a list detailing the numbers relevant to it.

The launch of Holland No 1 at the Vickers yard, Barrow-in-Furness.

	launched	builder
No 1	1901	All boats were
Nos 2–5	1902	built by Vickers
		Son & Maxim
Completion:	1901–3	

Specification

Displacement	surfaced:	104 tons
	submerged:	*No 1* 122 tons
		Nos 2–5 150 tons
Dimensions:		$63\frac{3}{4} \times 11\frac{3}{4} \times 10$ ft
Complement:		7
Propulsion	surfaced:	Single 4 cyl petrol engine;
		No 1 160 hp, *Nos 2–5* 250 hp
	submerged:	Single electric motor 74 hp
Speed	surfaced:	8 knots
	submerged:	5 knots
Range:		500 nm
Armament	Gun:	see armament note
	Torpedo:	Single 14 in bow tube

Class note: With this new branch of the Service and a new type of vessel there were numerous teething troubles, but by determination and trial and error the crews became accustomed to their boats and efficiency constantly improved. In exercises, many a captain of a super-Dreadnought was exceedingly surprised to find that a 'torpedo' had struck his ship without him even having been aware that a submarine was in the offing.

The Class was completed without periscopes; Capt R. Bacon, RN, devised a vertical telescope which fulfilled the purpose.

As trials continued and from constant use, ideas for improvement influenced the design of the A Class.

In the same period the USN Adder Class, also designed by Holland, had a range of 800 nm.

No 4 was used as gunnery target on 17 October 1912.
No 5 was lost while under tow on 8 August 1912.
None of the Class remained in service by 1913.

Armament note: The Class was designed to have an 8 in 'aerial gun' at the bow above the torpedo tube. The gun was to be $11\frac{1}{4}$ ft long, with a range of 1 mile, and fire a 22 lb projectile from a 100 lb gun-cotton charge. There is no evidence that it was fitted.

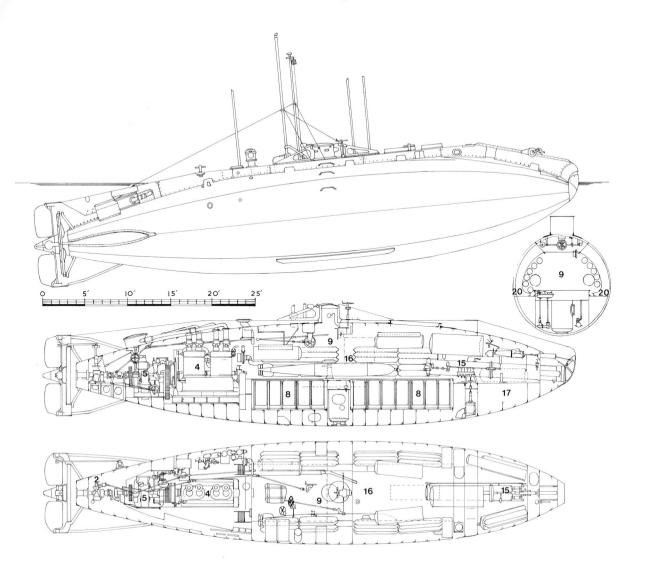

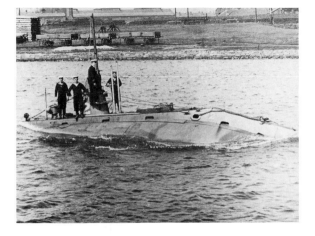

2 STEERING GEAR COMPARTMENT	15 FORWARD TORPEDO TUBE
4 MAIN ENGINE	16 TORPEDO STOWAGE
5 MAIN MOTOR	17 FUEL TANK
8 BATTERY SPACE	20 MAIN BALLAST TANK
9 CONTROL ROOM	

A posed photograph of Holland No 2 running on the surface, with her crew in their best shore-going rig.

A4 on builder's trials. Note the inch gauge on the bow, to aid trimming, and the rig of the crew.

	launched	builder
A1	1902	The complete Class
A2–A4	1903	was built by Vickers at
A5–A6	1904	Barrow-in-Furness
A7–13	1905	
A14 became *B1*		
Completion:	1903–5	

Specification

Displacement	surfaced:	*A1–A4* 165 tons
		A5–A14 180 tons
	submerged:	*A1–A4* 180 tons
		A5–A14 207 tons
Dimensions:		*A1–A4* 100 × 11½ × 11½ ft
		A5–14 99 × 12½ × 11½ ft
Complement:		11–14
Propulsion	surfaced:	*A1–A4* single 12 cyl petrol engine 500 hp
		A5–A12 and *A14* single 16 cyl petrol engine 550 hp
		A13 single heavy oil engine
	submerged:	*A1–A14* single electric motor 150 hp
Speed	surfaced:	11 knots (*A13* 10 knots; range 310 miles)
	submerged:	7 knots
Armament	Torpedo:	*A1* single 18 in bow tube
		A2–A14 two 18 in bow tubes

Class note: This was the first Admiralty-designed submarine. It was the first Class to have a conning tower (not included in the Holland Class), which was of great advantage in navigation, ship handling and pilotage, and gave increased visibility when the boat was on the surface.

Losses

A1 was the first Royal Navy submarine to be lost in peace or war. She sank after collision with SS *Berwick Castle* on 18 March 1904; she was salvaged and recommissioned but again sank, with further loss of life, while on trials in August 1911.

A2 foundered after grounding in Bomb Ketch Lake, Portsmouth, in January 1920.

A3 sank after collision with HMS *Hazard* on 2 February 1912. She was raised and used as a target, finally sinking in May 1912.

A4 sank after collision in harbour at Devonport in 1905.

A7 dived into the mud and was trapped in White Sand Bay on 16 January 1914.

A8 sank in Plymouth Sound on 8 June 1905, but was salvaged.

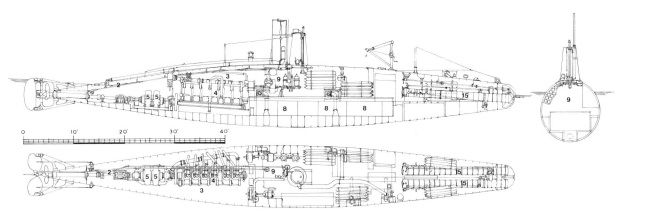

2 STEERING GEAR COMPARTMENT
3 MAIN ENGINE ROOM
4 MAIN ENGINE
5 MAIN MOTOR

8 BATTERY SPACE
9 CONTROL ROOM
15 FORWARD TORPEDO TUBES

A1. The canvas dodgers are missing from the conning tower, aft of which the compass binnacle can be seen below and behind the 'scaffolding' lookout position.

B4 on builder's trials. Note the ventilator on the conning tower.

	launched	builder
B1 (ex A14)	1904	The complete Class
B2–B7	1905	was built by Vickers
B8–B11	1906	at Barrow-in-Furness
Completion:	1905–6	

Specification

Displacement	surfaced:	280 tons
	submerged:	313 tons
Dimensions:		$135 \times 13\frac{1}{2} \times 12$ ft
Complement:		16
Propulsion	surfaced:	Single 16 cyl petrol engine 600 hp
	submerged:	Single electric motor 180 hp Fuel capacity 15 tons
Speed	surfaced:	13 knots
	submerged:	8 knots
Range	surfaced:	1000 nm at $8\frac{1}{2}$ knots
Armament	Torpedo:	Two 18 in bow tubes

Class note: This Class was the first Royal Navy submarine to be fitted with forward hydroplanes.

In the latter part of World War I, B6, B7, B8, B9 and 11 were extensively modified for surface use as patrol boats. The electric motor and conning tower were removed, the deck level raised and a wheelhouse added. They were re-designated S6–S10 and saw service in the Mediterranean.

Losses

B2 was sunk in collision in the Strait of Dover by SS *Amerika* on 14 October 1912.

B10 was destroyed by bombing while under repair in Venice dockyard on 9 August 1916.

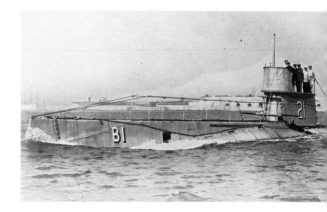

B1 leaving harbour with the casing party on the conning tower and the periscope raised.

The launch of C3. Note the forward hydroplanes and the riveting round the lower bow and the bilge keels.

	launched	builder
C1–C6	1906	
C7–C12	1907	C1–C16
C13	1908	Vickers,
C14	1907	Barrow-in-Furness
C15, C16	1908	
C17–C20	1908	HM Dockyard, Chatham
C21–C24	1908	Vickers,
C25-C32	1909	Barrow-in-Furness
C33, C34	1909	HM Dockyard, Chatham
C35, C36	1909	Vickers,
C37, C38	1910	Barrow-in-Furness
Completion:	1906–10	

Specification

Displacement	surfaced:	290 tons
	submerged:	320 tons
Dimensions:		135 × 13½ × 12 ft
Complement:		16
Propulsion	surfaced:	Single 16 cyl petrol engine 600 hp
	submerged:	Single electric motor 200 hp
Speed	surfaced:	13 knots
	submerged:	8 knots
Range	surfaced:	1500 nm at 8½ knots
Armament	Torpedo:	Two 18 in bow tubes

Class note: As they came to be refitted, the Class was fitted with W/T. The periscopes were increased in length and two were fitted.

Losses

C3 was used to blow up the Mole at Zeebrugge on 23 April 1918.*

C11 was in collision with SS *Eddystone* off Cromer on 14 July 1909.

C14 was in collision with Hopper No 29 in Plymouth Sound on 10 December 1913. She was salvaged.

C26 and *C27* were scuttled in Helsingfors Bay on 4 April 1918.†

C29 was mined in the North Sea on 29 August 1915.

C31 foundered, cause unknown, off the Belgian coast on 4 January 1915.

C32 went aground in the Gulf of Riga on 24 October 1917 and was destroyed by own forces.

C33 failed to return from patrol in the North Sea and is believed to have been lost on 4 August 1915.

C34 was torpedoed by *U-52* off the Shetland Isles on 21 July 1917.

C35 was scuttled in Helsingfors Bay on 5 April 1918.†

*C3's bows were filled with explosive with which she rammed the Mole. Her Captain was awarded the VC.

†The loss of these three boats and four of the E Class was a result of the German–Russian armistice in December 1917 and the Peace Treaty between Germany and Finland on 7 March 1918, which required that the British Baltic submarine flotilla should be handed over to the Germans. The flotilla had been very successful in sinking German shipping carrying Swedish iron ore for the German war machine. To avoid this surrender the Commanding Officer arranged that all his boats should be scuttled and their crews brought ashore.

D6 running on the surface, the watch in their white submarine jerseys indulging in semaphore practice.

	launched	builder
D1	1908	Vickers, Barrow-in-Furness

Specification

Displacement	surfaced:	550 tons
	submerged:	595 tons
Dimensions:		$162 \times 20\frac{1}{2} \times 14$ ft
Complement:		25
Propulsion	surfaced:	Single petrol engine 565 hp
	submerged:	Single electric motor 275 hp
Speed	surfaced:	16 knots
	submerged:	9 knots
Armament	Torpedo:	Three 18 in tubes, two bow, one stern

	launched	builder
D2–D4	1910	Vickers, Barrow-in-Furness
D5	1911	Vickers, Barrow-in-Furness
D6	1912	Vickers, Barrow-in-Furness
D7, D8	1912	HM Dockyard, Chatham

Specification

Displacement	surfaced:	604 tons
	submerged:	620 tons
Dimensions:		$162 \times 20\frac{1}{2} \times 14$ ft
Complement:		25
Propulsion	surfaced:	Two diesel engines 1200 hp
	submerged:	Two electric motors 550 hp
Speed	surfaced:	16 knots
	submerged:	9 knots
Range	surfaced:	2,500 nm at 10 knots
Armament	Gun:	D4 Single 4 in (see armament note); D5–D8 were fitted with one or two 12 pdrs when they were re-fitted
	Torpedo:	Three 18 in tubes, two bow, one stern

D6 cruising, her pennant number prominent.

Class note: This Class incorporated saddle tanks in lieu of internal ballast tanks. The conning tower was larger than any previous Class. They were the first boats designed to incorporate a W/T system, though the wireless mast had to be raised and lowered by hand.

During Fleet manoeuvres in 1910, *D1* successfully 'torpedoed' two 'enemy' cruisers—an augury of events in the coming war.

Armament note: This Class was the first to be armed on deck. *D4* had one 12 pdr mounted in a housing which could be retracted into the conning tower, using compressed air. No shell magazine was fitted.

Losses
D1 was sunk in target practice on 23 October 1918.
D2 was sunk by gunfire from a German patrol vessel off the Ems Estuary on 25 November 1914.
D3 sank after being bombed in error by a French airship on 15 March 1918.
D5 was mined off Great Yarmouth on 3 November 1914.
D6 was torpedoed by *UB-73* off the coast of Ulster on 28 June 1918.

The launch of D1 at Barrow-in-Furness.

E20 in harbour with the majority of her crew. Note the draught marks on the saddle tank, a miniature boat boom on the side of the casing, and the gun partially elevated.

	launched	builder
Group 1		
E1, *E2* (ex *D9*, *D10*)	1912	HM Dockyard, Chatham
E3–E6	1912	Vickers, Barrow-in-Furness
Completion:	1913	

Specification

Displacement	surfaced:	660 tons
	submerged:	810 tons
Dimensions:		176 bp × 22½ × 12 ft
Complement:		30
Propulsion	surfaced:	Two diesel engines 1,600 hp
	submerged:	Two electric motors 840 hp
		Fuel capacity 45 tons
Speed	surfaced:	16 knots
	submerged:	10 knots
Range	surfaced:	3,000 nm at 10 knots
Armament	Gun:	Single 6 pdr or 4 in (see armament note)
	Torpedo:	Four 18 in, two bow, two beam (see armament note)

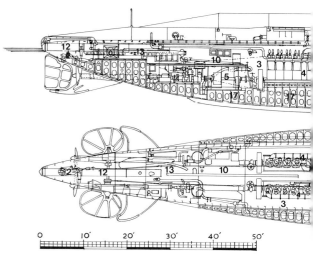

Group 2	launched	builder
E7, E8	1912	HM Dockyard, Chatham
E9, E10	1913	Vickers, Barrow-in-Furness
E11	1914	Vickers, Barrow-in-Furness
E12–E13	1913	HM Dockyard, Chatham
E14–E16	1914	Vickers, Barrow-in-Furness
E17–E21	1915	Vickers, Barrow-in-Furness

Group 3		
E22–E24	1915	Vickers, Barrow-in-Furness
E25	1915	Beardmore
E26	1916	Beardmore
E27	1916	Yarrow
E29, E30	1916	Armstrong
E31	1916	Scotts
E32	1916	White
E33, E34	1916	Thornycroft
E35, E36	1916	John Brown
E37, E38	1916	Fairfield
E39, E40	1916	Palmer
E41, E42	1915	Cammell Laird
E43, E44	1916	Swan Hunter
E45, E46	1916	Cammell Laird
E47	1916	Fairfield (completed by Beardmore)

	launched	builder
E48	1917	Fairfield (completed by Beardmore)
E49	1917	Swan Hunter
E50	1917	John Brown
E51	1916	Scotts
E52	1917	Denny
E53	1916	Beardmore
E54	1917	Beardmore
E55, E56	1917	Denny
Completion:	1913–17	

Specification as Group 1 except:
Displacement surfaced: 662 tons
submerged: 835 tons
Dimensions: $181 \times 23\frac{1}{2} \times 12\frac{1}{2}$ ft
Armament E7 and E8 as Group 1; E9 onwards:
Torpedo: Five 18 in tubes, two bow, two beam, one stern (see armament note)
Mines: E24, E34, E41, E45, E46, E51 were converted for minelaying. The beam tubes were omitted and they had capacity for 20 mines

1 TRIMMING TANK
2 STEERING GEAR COMPARTMENT
3 MAIN ENGINE ROOM
4 MAIN ENGINE
5 MAIN MOTOR
8 BATTERY SPACE
9 CONTROL ROOM
10 CREW ACCOMMODATION
11 WARD ROOM
12 AFTER TORPEDO TUBES
13 AFTER TORPEDO STOWAGE
14 BEAM TORPEDO TUBES
15 FORWARD TORPEDO TUBES
16 FORWARD TORPEDO STOWAGE
17 FUEL TANKS

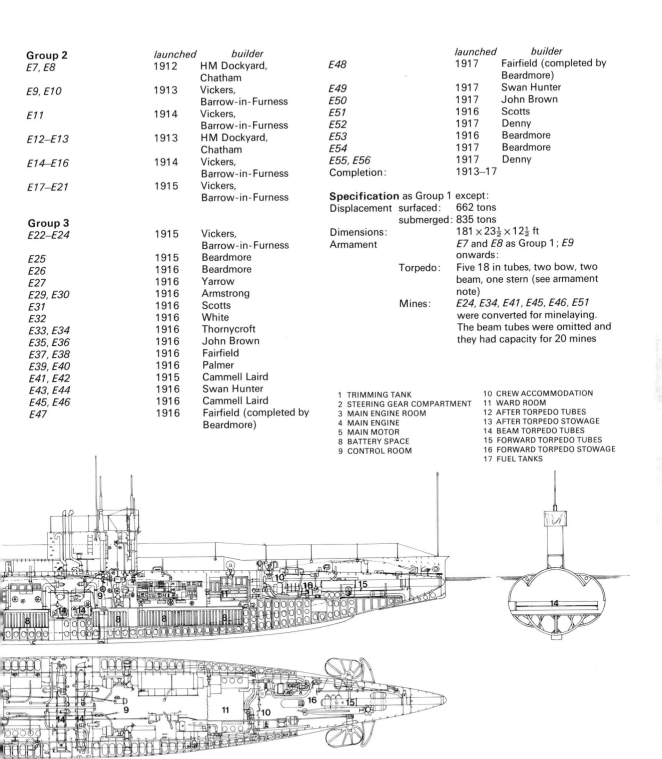

E CLASS (continued)

E6 outward bound on a glassy sea showing the resistance created by this form of bow. The saddle tanks are visible below and aft of the conning tower due to the speed of the boat.

Class note: *E28* was cancelled. *E25* and *E26* were ordered by the Turkish Government, but were retained by the Royal Navy.

Armament note: From the E Class onwards all submarines were built with one or more magazines for gun ammunition. No standard weapon had been decided upon. For example, *E19* had one 2 pdr; *E20* had a 6 in howitzer; *E21* had both a 12 and a 2 pdr, the latter being portable and stowed inside the boat; *E11* had one 6 pdr, and *E12* a single 4 in gun.

Losses

E4 and *E41* were in collision off Harwich on 15 August 1916. *E4* was submerged and *E41* cruising on the surface when the accident occurred; there was great loss of life. Both boats were salvaged, recommissioned in May 1917, and continued in service for the remainder of the war.

E1, *E8*, *E9* and *E19* were scuttled in Hesingfors Bay on 3–4 April 1918. See footnote, p. 21

E3 was lost on 18 October 1914. One account states that she was torpedoed by *U-27* in the North Sea; another that she was sunk by SMS *Strassburg* in the Heligoland Bight.

E5 was lost, reason unknown, in the North Sea on or after 7 March 1916.

E6 was mined on 26 December 1915 in the North Sea.

E7 was blown up by Turkish forces after becoming trapped in anti-submarine nets in the Dardanelles.

E10 was lost, cause unknown, in the North Sea on or after 18 January 1915.

E13 was interned by the Danish authorities on 18 August 1915 after running aground at Saltholm while under fire from German destroyers.

E14 was mined in the Dardanelles on 22 January 1918.

E15 ran aground at Kephez Point in the Dardanelles on 15 April 1915. To avoid capture by the Turks she was torpedoed by picket boats from HMS *Majestic* and *Triumph*.

E16 was mined off the Heligoland Bight on 22 August 1916.

E17 ran aground and was wrecked in the Texel estuary on 6 January 1916.

E18 was sunk in a surface action on 24 May 1916 with SMS '*K*' (the equivalent of a British 'Q ship') in the Baltic.

E20 was torpedoed by *UB-15* in the Sea of Marmara on 5 November 1915.*

E22 was torpedoed by *UB-18* in the North Sea on 25 April 1916.

E24 was mined in the North Sea on 24 March 1916.

E26 was lost, reason unknown, in the North Sea on 6 July 1916.

E30 was lost, reason unknown, in the North Sea on or after 22 November 1916.

E34 was mined in the North Sea on 20 July 1918.

E36 was lost, reason unknown, in the North Sea on or after 17 January 1917.

E37 was lost, reason unknown, in the North Sea on or after 1 December 1916.

E47 was lost, reason unknown, in the North Sea on or after 20 August, 1917.

E49 was mined and sank off the Shetlands on 12 March 1917.

E50 was mined and sank in the North Sea on 1 February 1918.

*The loss of *E20* was an unfortunate example of Anglo–French co-operation during World War I. *E20* was to have rendezvoused with the French submarine *Turquoise* for a joint patrol in the Bosphorus, but she ran aground and surrendered to the Turkish naval forces. Her CO made no attempt to destroy his confidential books and signals, which the Germans acquired and of which they took full advantage. In consequence *UB-15* was waiting for *E20* and torpedoed her.

F2 running on the surface with both periscopes raised. The radio aerial is the long-wire used on submarines until the 1950s.

	launched	builder
F1	1914	HM Dockyard, Chatham
F2	1914	White
F3	1915	Thornycroft

Cancellations: *F4–58* were projected but cancelled.
Completion: 1915–17

Specification

Displacement	surfaced:	353 tons
	submerged:	525 tons
Dimensions:		$151 \times 16 \times 10\frac{1}{2}$ ft
Complement:		18–20
Propulsion	surfaced:	Two diesel engines 900 hp
	submerged:	Two electric motors 400 hp
Speed	surfaced:	$14\frac{1}{2}$ knots
	submerged:	9 knots
Range	surfaced:	3,000 nm at 9 knots
		Fuel capacity: $17\frac{1}{2}$ tons
Armament	Gun:	Single 2 pdr
	Torpedo:	Three 18 in tubes, two bow, one stern

Note: The boats of this Class were to an Admiralty design for a coastal submarine and it is not surprising that the lead boat, *F1*, was built at HM Dockyard, Chatham.

Rumour prevails that the Fs were based on the Vickers 'V' design for a coastal boat but design improvements included a stern torpedo tube, larger hydroplanes and more effective plane guards.

The 'F' boats were found to be less buoyant than the 'V' but all in all were quite comparable. Both Classes were fitted with self-compensating fuel tanks.

There were no war losses.

V3 on basin trials with a canvas dodger which appears to have been tailored to fit.

	launched	builder
V1	1914	Vickers, Barrow-in-Furness
V2–V4	1915	Vickers, Barrow-in-Furness
Completion:	1914–16	

Specification

Displacement	surfaced:	364 tons
	submerged:	486 tons
Dimensions:		148 × 16 × 11 ft
Complement:		18
Propulsion	surfaced:	Two diesel engines 900 hp
	submerged:	Two electric motors 380 hp
Speed	surfaced:	14 knots
	submerged:	9 knots
Range	surfaced:	3,000 nm at 9 knots
Armament	Gun:	Single 2 pdr
	Torpedo:	Two 18 in tubes, bow only

Class note: In extremis it was not unkown for the CO of a submarine needing extra speed to connect the electric motors as well as the diesels to the shafts whilst on the surface. This could be done for a comparatively short time as, with both methods of propulsion in use, the batteries quickly lost their charge and the diesels were not able to re-charge them.

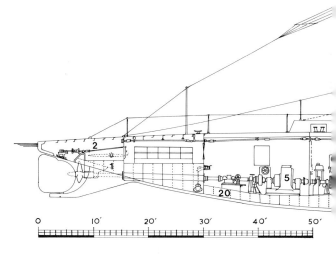

1 TRIMMING TANK	10 CREW ACCOMMODATION	
2 STEERING GEAR COMPARTMENT	15 FORWARD TORPEDO TUBES	
3 MAIN ENGINE ROOM	16 FORWARD TORPEDO STOWAGE	
4 MAIN ENGINE	17 FUEL TANKS	
5 MAIN MOTOR	20 MAIN BALLAST TANK	
8 BATTERY SPACE	25 SEARCH PERISCOPE	
9 CONTROL ROOM	26 ATTACK PERISCOPE	
	27 W/T MAST	

V1 at her mooring in the dockyard after commissioning. The plethora of radio aerials is extraordinary, as also are the safety rails. These were presumably fitted for basin trials as it is doubtful if she would go to sea with so much 'fencing' to create resistance.

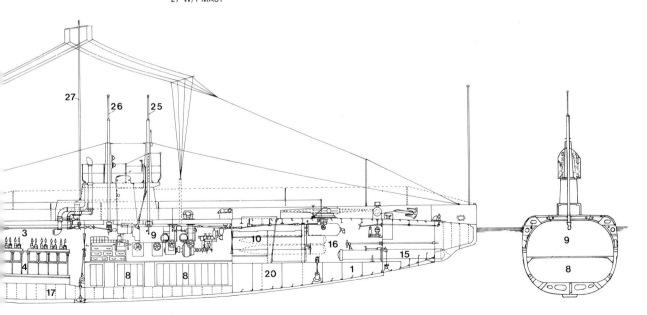

An S Class boat built in the UK for the Italian Navy. The boat, although looking a little woe-begone, is on trials in the Clyde.

	launched	builder
S1, S2	1914	Scotts

Specification

Displacement	surfaced:	265 tons
	submerged:	324 tons
Dimensions:		$148\frac{1}{2} \times 14 \times 9\frac{1}{2}$ ft
Complement:		18–21
Propulsion	surfaced:	Two diesel engines 600 hp
	submerged:	Electric motors 400 hp
		Two shafts
Range	surfaced:	1600 nm at $8\frac{1}{2}$ knots
	submerged:	75 nm at $5\frac{1}{2}$ knots
Armament	Gun:	Single quick-firing
	Torpedo:	Two 18 in bow tubes

Class note: This Class was also known as the Scott-Laurenti type. They were built to an Italian design, for whose navy they were originally intended. They were commissioned into the Royal Navy and served with the 4th and 8th submarine flotillas until October 1915. S3, from the same builder, was launched in 1915 but not commissioned into the Royal Navy. All three boats were then passed over to the Italian Navy.

S1 in dry dock at Scotts yard, presumably after trials. The flat stern appears to have been renewed.

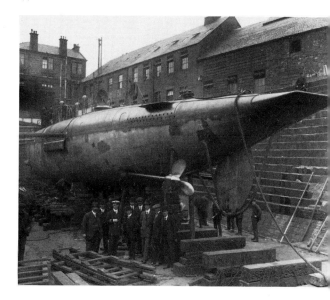

	launched	builder
W1	1914	Armstrong
W2–W4	1915	Armstrong

Specification

Displacement	surfaced:	*W1, W2* 331 tons
		W3, W4 320 tons
	submerged:	*W1, W2* 499 tons
		W3, W4 490 tons
Dimensions:		*W1, W2* $171\frac{1}{2} \times 15\frac{1}{2} \times 9$ ft
		W3, W4 $149\frac{1}{2} \times 17 \times 9\frac{1}{2}$ ft
Complement:		19
Propulsion	surfaced:	*W1, W2* two diesel engines 750 hp
		W3, W4 two diesel engines 700 hp
	submerged:	Two electric motors 480 hp
Speed	surfaced:	13 knots
	submerged:	8 knots
Range	surfaced:	2,500 nm at 8 knots
	submerged:	65 nm at 5 knots
Armament	Gun:	Single 3 in
	Torpedo:	Two 18 in tubes (see armament note)

W4, probably entering harbour. She is wearing the Royal Italian Navy ensign.

Class note: The Class was known as the Armstrong-Laubeuf type, having been built in the UK for the Italian Navy. *W1* and *W2* were commissioned into the Royal Navy and served in the 10th submarine flotilla until *W3* and *W4* were completed in August 1916. All four were then transferred to the Italian Navy.

Armament note: *W1* and *W2* were fitted with four torpedo tubes, two on each beam. They were angled forward on 'drop frames' fitted to the external casing below the water line.

	launched	builder
G1	1914	HM Dockyard, Chatham
G2–G5	1915	HM Dockyard, Chatham
G6, G7	1915	Armstrong
G8–13	1916	Vickers
G14	1916	Scotts
Completion:	1915–17	

Specification

Displacement	surfaced:	700 tons
	submerged:	975 tons
Dimensions:		$187 \times 22\frac{1}{2} \times 13\frac{1}{2}$ ft
Complement:		31
Propulsion	surfaced:	Two diesel engines 1,600 hp
	submerged:	Two electric motors 840 hp
		Fuel capacity 44 tons
Speed	surfaced:	$14\frac{1}{2}$ knots
	submerged:	10 knots
Range	surfaced:	2,400 nm at 12 knots
Armament	Gun:	Single 3 in (see armament note)
	Torpedo:	Four 18 in tubes, two bow, two beam
		One 21 in stern tube

G8 in commission with enhanced armament of a 3 pdr gun aft of the conning tower.

Armament note: These were the first Royal Naval submarines to be armed with the 21 in torpedo. The Class was normally intended to carry one 12 pdr and one 2 pdr portable gun.

Losses

G7 was lost due to enemy action on 1 November 1918 in the North Sea.

G8 was lost on 14 January 1918, or thereafter, in the North Sea, reason unknown.

G9 was attacked on 16 September 1917 and sunk in error by HMS *Petard* off the Norwegian coast.

G11 ran aground and was wrecked while entering Harwich harbour on 22 November 1918.

G10 on the surface with her radio masts vertical, the duty watch on the conning tower and a canvas cover on the breech of her 3 in gun.

	launched	builder
Nautilus	1914	Vickers, Barrow-in-Furness
Completed:	1917	

Specification

Displacement	surfaced:	1, 270 tons
	submerged:	1,694 tons
Dimensions:		$242\frac{1}{2} \times 26 \times 16$ ft
Propulsion	surfaced:	Two diesel engines 3,700 hp
	submerged:	Two electric motors, 1,000 hp
Speed	surfaced:	17 knots
	submerged:	10 knots
Range	surfaced:	5,000 nm at 10 knots
Armament	Gun:	Single 12 pdr (one 3 in DP/HA gun on commissioning)
	Torpedo:	Six 18 in bow tubes

Class notes: This experimental boat was designed for long-range use. It suffered many teething troubles and did not become operational.

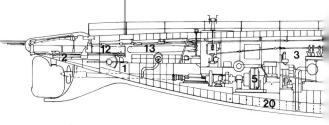

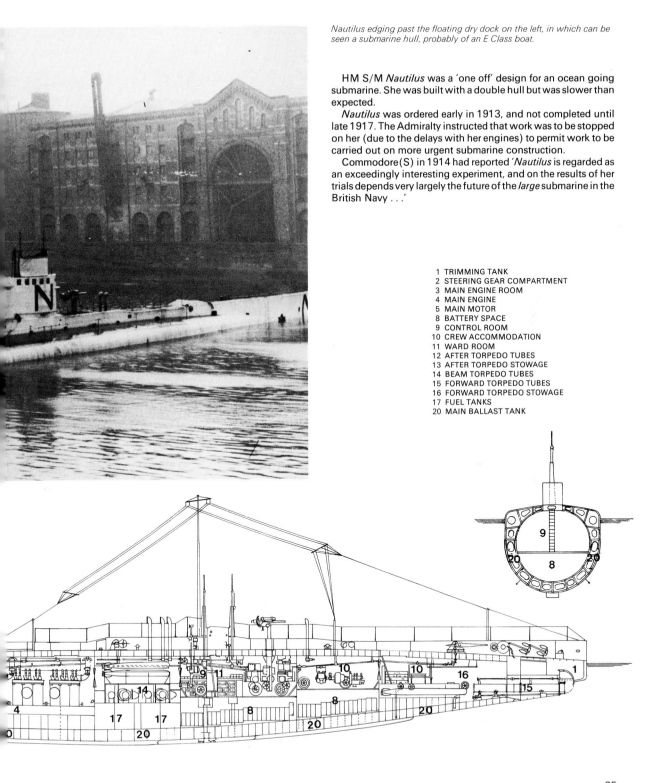

Nautilus edging past the floating dry dock on the left, in which can be seen a submarine hull, probably of an E Class boat.

HM S/M *Nautilus* was a 'one off' design for an ocean going submarine. She was built with a double hull but was slower than expected.

Nautilus was ordered early in 1913, and not completed until late 1917. The Admiralty instructed that work was to be stopped on her (due to the delays with her engines) to permit work to be carried out on more urgent submarine construction.

Commodore(S) in 1914 had reported '*Nautilus* is regarded as an exceedingly interesting experiment, and on the results of her trials depends very largely the future of the *large* submarine in the British Navy . . .'

1 TRIMMING TANK
2 STEERING GEAR COMPARTMENT
3 MAIN ENGINE ROOM
4 MAIN ENGINE
5 MAIN MOTOR
8 BATTERY SPACE
9 CONTROL ROOM
10 CREW ACCOMMODATION
11 WARD ROOM
12 AFTER TORPEDO TUBES
13 AFTER TORPEDO STOWAGE
14 BEAM TORPEDO TUBES
15 FORWARD TORPEDO TUBES
16 FORWARD TORPEDO STOWAGE
17 FUEL TANKS
20 MAIN BALLAST TANK

A Group 2 boat of H Class leaving for trials after commissioning.

	launched	builder
Group 1		
H1–H10	1915	Canadian Vickers
*H11, H12**	1917	Fore River Plant, Quincy, Mass, USA

Specification

Displacement	surfaced:	364 tons
	submerged:	434 tons
Dimensions:		$150 \times 15\frac{1}{2} \times 12\frac{1}{2}$ ft
Propulsion	surfaced:	Two diesel engines 480 hp
	submerged:	Two electric motors 320 hp
		Fuel capacity 16 tons
Speed	surfaced:	13 knots
	submerged:	11 knots
Armament	Torpedo:	Four 18 in bow tubes

Group 2		
H21, H22	1917	Vickers
H23	1918	Vickers
H24	1917	Vickers
H25	1918	Vickers
H26	1917	Vickers
H27–H32	1918	Vickers
H33, H34	1918	Cammell Laird
H41, H42	1918	Armstrong
H43, H44	1919	Armstrong
H47	1918	Beardmore
H48–50	1919	Beardmore
H51	1918	HM Dockyard, Pembroke
H52	1919	HM Dockyard, Pembroke

Cancellations: The following boats were cancelled in 1917:
H35–40 (Cammell Laird); *H45, H46* (Armstrong); *H53, H54*
(HM Dockyard, Devonport).

Specification

Displacement	surfaced:	440 tons
	submerged:	500 tons
Dimensions:		$171 \times 15\frac{1}{2} \times 14$ ft
Complement:		22
Propulsion:		As Group 1
Speed		As Group 1
Range	surfaced:	1,600 nm at 10 knots
Armament	Gun:	Single 12 pdr (some boats only)
	Torpedo:	Four 21 in bow tubes

* These two boats were not delivered until the United States entered the
war. *H15–H20* were built but not delivered.

1	TRIMMING TANK	15	FORWARD TORPEDO TUBES
3	MAIN ENGINE ROOM	16	FORWARD TORPEDO STOWAGE
4	MAIN ENGINE	17	FUEL TANKS
5	MAIN MOTOR	19	RADIO ROOM
8	BATTERY SPACE	20	MAIN BALLAST TANK
9	CONTROL ROOM	25	SEARCH PERISCOPE
10	CREW ACCOMMODATION	26	ATTACK PERISCOPE
11	WARD ROOM	27	RADIO MAST

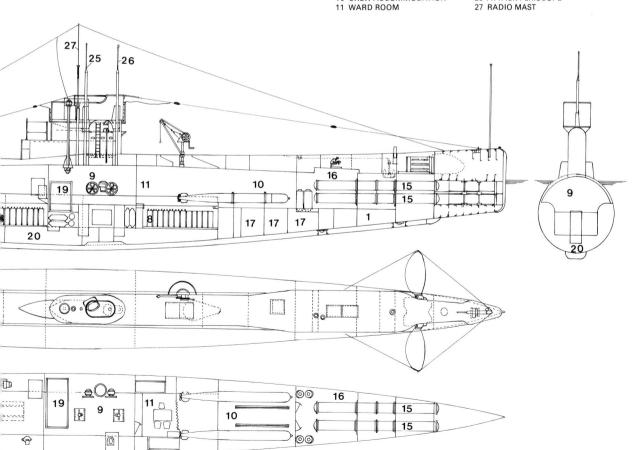

H42 with the casing party manoeuvring a torpedo for stowage below.

Losses

H3 was mined off Cattaro in the Adriatic Sea on 15 July 1916.

H4 foundered in the English Channel on 3 September 1913. She was salvaged and used as a target in the following year.

H5 was lost in collision in the Irish Sea on 6 March 1918.

H6 was interned by the Netherlands Navy on 8 January 1916 after stranding on Schiermonnikoog. In February 1916 she was salvaged and purchased by the Netherlands Navy who commissioned her as *O8*. In 1940, as a result of the German occupation of Holland, she was scuttled at Dan Helder but again salvaged and commissioned into the German navy as *UD1*. She served as an operational U-boat until March 1943. On 3 May 1945 she was scuttled for the second time and later broken up at Kiel.

H10 was lost, reason unknown, on or after 19 January 1918 in the North Sea.

H29 sank in Devonport dockyard in August 1926.

H31 was mined in the Bay of Biscay on 24 December 1941.

H42 sank after a collision with the destroyer HMS *Versatile* off Gibraltar on 23 March 1922.

H47 sank after collision with *L12* off the Welsh coast on 9 July 1929.

H49 was torpedoed by German E-boats off the Dutch coast on 27 October 1940.

J5 entering harbour. Note the 3 in gun at full depression, and the forward hydroplane in its recess.

	launched	builder
J1, J2	1915	HM Dockyard, Portsmouth
J3 (ex *J7*)	1915	HM Dockyard, Pembroke
J4 (ex *J8*)	1916	HM Dockyard, Pembroke
J5, J6	1915	HM Dockyard, Devonport
J7	1917	HM Dockyard, Devonport

Class note: Boats of this Class were the forerunners of the K Class, but diesel powered. It will be noticed from the illustrations that the bow shape is similar.

Armament note: As designed, J Class submarines had one 3 in DP/HA and one 2 pdr portable gun, but a 4 in gun was mounted on some of the Class.

Loss

J6 was mistaken for a U-boat and sunk by gunfire by the 'Q' ship *Cymric* off Blyth, Northumberland, on 15 October 1918.

Specification

Displacement	surfaced:	1,210 tons (*J7* 1,260 tons)
	submerged:	1,820 tons (*J7* 1,826 tons)
Dimensions:		$275\frac{1}{2} \times 23 \times 16$ ft
Complement:		44
Propulsion	surfaced:	Three diesel engines 3,600 hp
	submerged:	Three electric motors 1,400 hp
		Fuel capacity 80 tons
Speed	surfaced:	$19\frac{1}{2}$ knots
	submerged:	$9\frac{1}{2}$ knots
Range	surfaced:	5,000 nm at $12\frac{1}{2}$ knots
Armament	Gun:	One or two 3 or 4 in mounted at the same level as the conning tower but on separate platform (see armament note)
	Torpedo:	Six 18 in tubes; four bow, two beam

SWORDFISH CLASS

		launched	builder
Swordfish (later *S1*, then again *Swordfish*)		1916	Scotts

Specification

Displacement	surfaced:	932 tons
	submerged:	1,470 tons
Dimensions:		$231\frac{1}{4} \times 23 \times 14\frac{1}{2}$ ft
Propulsion	surfaced:	Steam turbine 3,750 hp
	submerged:	Two electric motors (1,400 hp
		Two shafts
Speed	surfaced:	18 knots
	submerged:	10 knots
Armament	Gun:	Nil (see armament note)
	Torpedo:	Two 21 in and four 18 in tubes

Armament note: *Swordfish* was designed to have two 3 in DP/HA guns on single disappearing mountings.

Note: This experimental steam turbine powered submarine, the predecessor of the K Class, was a further development of the diesel powered J Class (which was faster on the surface than *Swordfish*) in the attempt to find an ideal design for a fleet, as distinct from a patrol, submarine.

The Admiralty intended then, and the theory still lingers, that submarines should form an integral part of the battle fleet. Therefore they had to have the speed to keep up with the surface ships. Even on the surface that was difficult, and there was the added hazard that submarines, because of their size and low profile, were vulnerable to collision damage.

Swordfish was not a success and, after various trials, she was refitted as a surface patrol vessel. The major modifications were to remove the electric motors, add sheer to her bows to aid seaworthiness, and a wheelhouse. She was armed with two 12 pdr guns and served the rest of her short career creditably at Portsmouth.

Swordfish on trials. Compare the hull shape with the Italian S Class.

Swordfish with a 'bone in her teeth' as she makes speed, and smoke, on trials.

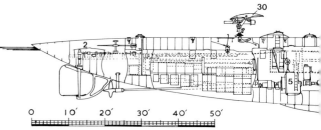

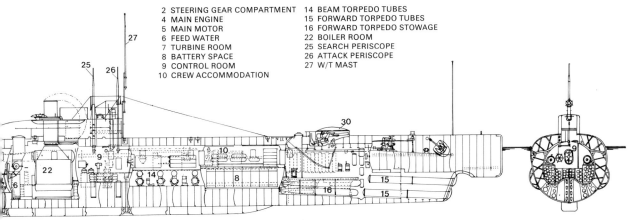

2 STEERING GEAR COMPARTMENT
4 MAIN ENGINE
5 MAIN MOTOR
6 FEED WATER
7 TURBINE ROOM
8 BATTERY SPACE
9 CONTROL ROOM
10 CREW ACCOMMODATION
14 BEAM TORPEDO TUBES
15 FORWARD TORPEDO TUBES
16 FORWARD TORPEDO STOWAGE
22 BOILER ROOM
25 SEARCH PERISCOPE
26 ATTACK PERISCOPE
27 W/T MAST

K3 leaving Barrow for trials.

	launched	builder
K1, K2	1916	HM Dockyard, Portsmouth
K3, K4	1916	Vickers
K5	1916	HM Dockyard, Portsmouth
K6, K7	1916	HM Dockyard, Devonport
K8–K10	1916	Vickers
K11	1916	Armstrong
K12	1917	Armstrong
K13 (later K22)	1916	Fairfield
K14	1917	Fairfield
K15	1917	Scotts
K16	1917	Beardmore
K17	1917	Vickers

Specification

Displacement	surfaced:	1,883 tons
	submerged:	2,600 tons
Dimensions:		$338 \times 26\frac{1}{2} \times 16$ ft
Complement:		55
Propulsion	surfaced:	Two steam geared turbines 10,000 hp diesel engine 800 hp (auxiliary)
	submerged:	Two electric motors 1,400 hp Fuel capacity 170 tons
Speed	surfaced:	24 knots
	submerged:	$9\frac{1}{2}$ knots
Armament	Gun:	Two 4 in single; one 3 in single AA; one Lewis gun (see armament note)
	Torpedo:	Eight 18 in tubes; four bow, four beam A depth charge thrower was mounted on some boats in the Class

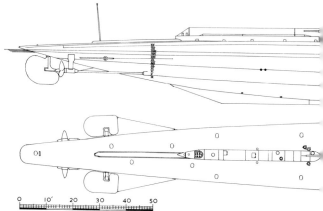

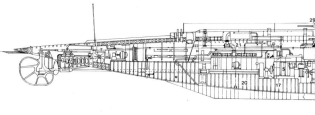

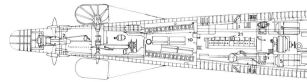

Class note: As mentioned under Swordfish Class, this design was intended to operate with the battle fleet; thus the reasons for the high surface speed and medium gun armament. After trials the height of the bow was raised to avoid a tendency in the earlier boats to trim by the bows. The change gave the extra buoyancy required, but also necessitated increasing the height of the conning tower.

Armament note: The Class was designed to be mounted with two 5.5 in guns on single mountings, but these were not fitted. It was also planned that the boats should have two 18 in torpedo tubes on a twin mounting on the upper casing for use in night attacks, but this was removed from all the boats.

1 TRIMMING TANK
2 STEERING GEAR COMPARTMENT
4 MAIN ENGINE
5 MAIN MOTOR
6 FEED WATER
7 TURBINE ROOM
8 BATTERY SPACE
9 CONTROL ROOM
10 CREW ACCOMMODATION
11 WARD ROOM
14 BEAM TORPEDO TUBES
15 FORWARD TORPEDO TUBES

16 FORWARD TORPEDO STOWAGE
17 FUEL TANKS
19 RADIO ROOM
20 MAIN BALLAST TANK
21 DIESEL ROOM
22 BOILER ROOM
25 SEARCH PERISCOPE
26 ATTACK PERISCOPE
27 W/T MAST
29 4 in GUN
30 3 in GUN

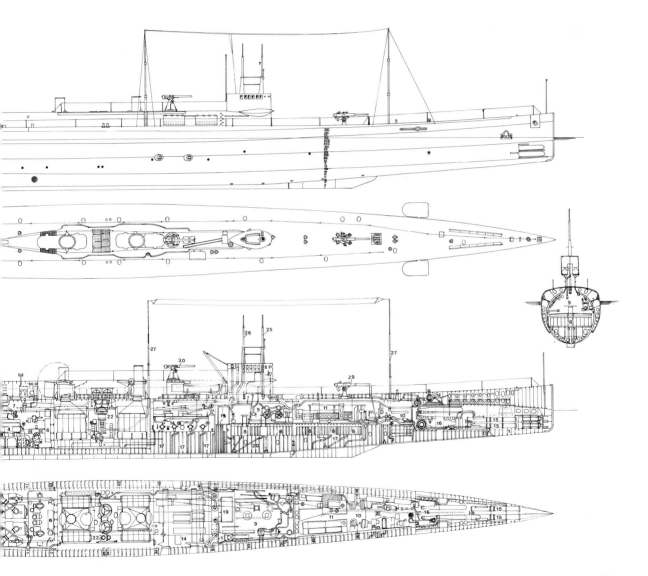

Losses

K1 collided with *K4* off the Danish coast on 18 November 1917. *K1* was badly damaged and her crew were taken off before she was sunk by gunfire from HMS *Blonde*.

K4 sank in collision with HMS *Inflexible* in a night exercise off May Island on 31 January 1918. The submarine, which was on the surface, altered course under the bows of the battleship.

K5 foundered in the Bay of Biscay on 20 January 1921.

K13 foundered in the Gare Loch while on builders trials on 29 January 1917. She was salvaged and renamed *K22* in March 1917.

K15 sank in Portsmouth harbour on 25 June 1921.

K17 was lost in the same night exercise as *K4* on 31 January 1918. She was rammed, after altering course, by HMS *Fearless* off May Island.

K6, showing the modified bow, open upper bridge above the conning tower, and the heightened funnels.

K26 during trials after World War I.

	launched	builder
K26	1919	Vickers (completed at HM Dockyard, Chatham)

Completion: September 1923

Cancellations: Five further boats on order were cancelled in November 1918. They were: *K23–K25* (Armstrong); *K27* and *K28* (Vickers)

Close up view of the conning tower of K26.

Specification

Displacement	surfaced:	2,140 tons
	submerged:	2,770 tons
Dimensions:		$351\frac{1}{4} \times 28 \times 16\frac{1}{2}$ ft
Complement:		58
Propulsion	surfaced:	Two steam geared turbines 10,000 hp
	submerged:	Two electric motors 1,400 hp
Speed	surfaced:	$23\frac{1}{2}$ knots
	submerged:	9 knots
Armament	Gun:	Three 4 in single (see armament note)
	Torpedo:	Six 21 in bow tubes; four 18 in beam tubes

Class notes: *K26* was planned to be the first of a 'follow up' to the earlier K Class. The hull was longer and she carried greater armament, but her machinery was the same. This had the understandable result that she was slower.

Armament note: The 4 in guns had 20 deg elevation and a range of 9,000 yds.

L71 preparing to enter harbour. She is a group 3 boat with 4 in guns fore and aft of the conning tower.

Group 1	launched	builder
L1 (ex E56), L2 (ex E57),		
L3, L4	1917	Vickers
L5	1918	Swan Hunter
L6	1918	Beardmore
L7, L8	1917	Cammell Laird

Specification

Displacement	surfaced:	890 tons
	submerged:	1,070 tons
Dimensions:		$231 \times 23\frac{1}{2} \times 14$ ft
Complement:		36
Propulsion	surfaced:	Two diesel engines 2,400 hp
	submerged:	Two electric motors 1,600 hp
		Fuel capacity 76 tons
Speed	surfaced:	$17\frac{1}{2}$ knots
	submerged:	$10\frac{1}{2}$ knots
Range	surfaced:	2,800 nm at 10 knots
Armament	Gun:	Single 3 or 4 in
	Torpedo:	Six 18 in; four bow, two beam

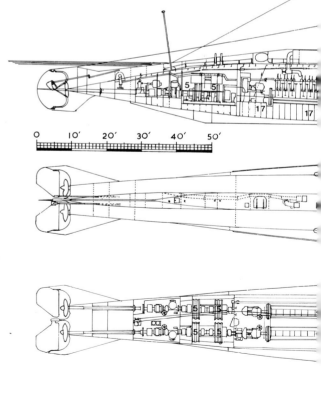

Group 2

	launched	*builder*
L9, L10	1918	Denny
L11, L12, L14	1918	Vickers
L15, L16	1918	Fairfield
L19, L18, L20	1918	Vickers
L19, L21–L27	1919	Vickers
L33	1919	Swan Hunter

Cancellations: L13, L36–L49 were not ordered. The following were cancelled in April 1919: L28–L31 (Vickers); L34 and L35 (HM Dockyard, Pembroke). L32 had been launched by Vickers, but was broken up

Completion: L23 was completed at HM Dockyard, Chatham; L26 at HM Dockyard, Portsmouth. L11, L12, L14, L17 and L25 were completed as minelayers

Specification as Group 1 except

Displacement	surfaced:	895 tons
	submerged:	1.075 tons
Dimensions:		$238\frac{1}{2} \times 23\frac{1}{2} \times 14$ ft

Armament (except Minelayers)
Gun:	Single 4 in
Torpedo:	Two 21 in bow tubes; two 18 in beam tubes

Armament (Minelayers)
Gun:	Single 4 in
Torpedo:	Four 21 in bow tubes
Mines:	14

3 MAIN ENGINE ROOM
4 MAIN ENGINE
5 MAIN MOTOR
8 BATTERY SPACE
9 CONTROL ROOM
10 CREW ACCOMMODATION
11 WARD ROOM

15 FORWARD TORPEDO TUBES
16 FORWARD TORPEDO STOWAGE
17 FUEL TANKS
25 SEARCH PERISCOPE
26 ATTACK PERISCOPE
27 W/T MAST
29 4 in GUN

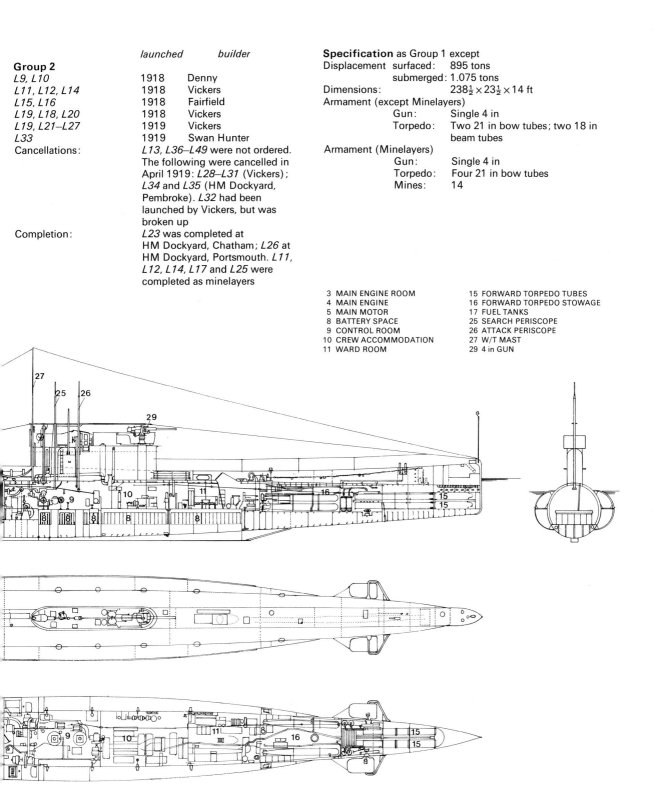

L20 leaving harbour, the casing crew stowing the mooring ropes. The anchor can be seen in its housing near the bow. The gun is slightly elevated.

	launched	builder
Group 3		
L52	1918	Armstrong
L53	1919	Armstrong
L54	1919	Denny
L55	1918	Fairfield
L56	1919	Fairfield
L69	1918	Beardmore
L71	1919	Scotts

Cancellations: The following were cancelled: *L50, L51, L60, L61* (Cammell Laird); *L57, L58, L62* (Fairfield); *L59, L70* (Beardmore); *L63, L64, L72* (Scotts); *L65, L66* (Swan Hunter); *L67, L68* (Armstrong); *L73, L74* (Denny)

Completion: *L53* was completed at HM Dockyard, Chatham, *L54* at HM Dockyard, Devonport; *L69* at HM Dockyard, Rosyth
L67 and *L68* were completed in 1927 for the Yugoslav government. They were named *Hrabri* and *Nebojsa*

L12 with her superimposed 4 in gun. The pronounced bulk of her saddle tanks shows clearly. Alongside H28 is an R Class attack submarine.

Specification

Displacement	surfaced:	960 tons
	submerged:	1,150 tons
Dimensions		235 × 23½ × 13 ft
Complement:		40
Propulsion	surfaced:	Two diesel engines 1,920 hp
	submerged:	Two electric motors, 1,150 hp
		Fuel capacity 76 tons
Speed	surfaced:	17 knots
	submerged:	10½ knots
Range	surfaced:	2,800 nm at 10 knots
Armament	Gun:	Two 4 in single
	Torpedo:	Six 21 in bow tubes

Class note: In the 1919 edition of *Jane's Fighting Ships* the comment is made that 'the L Class is in a highly complex state owing to the variations in build giving ten or more types by appearance'.

Armament note: *L1–L8* were designed to have two 3 in DP/HA guns, but were only fitted with one. *L11* had no deck gun. *L3, L12, L14, L17* and *L18* had one 4 in gun.

Losses

L9 foundered in Hong Kong harbour during a typhoon on 18 August 1923. She was salvaged.

L10 was sunk on 30 October 1918 by the German destroyer *S33* off the R. Texel.

L24 was in collision with HMS *Resolution* and sank off Portland on 10 January 1924.

L55 was forced into a minefield by the Bolshevik destroyers *Gavril* and *Azard* in the Baltic Sea on 4 June 1919, and was sunk by gunfire. She was salvaged and re-commissioned into the Soviet Navy in 1928 under her original number.

There were no war losses in this Class.

M1 leaving for sea trials with some dockyard staff on board. The 12 in gun is elevated to 30°.

		launched	builder
M1 (ex K18)		1917	Vickers
M2 (ex K19)		1918	Vickers
M3 (ex K20)		1918	Armstrong Whitworth
Cancellation:		M4 was not completed, but sold back to Armstrong Whitworth for scrap	

Specification

Displacement	surfaced:	1,600 tons
	submerged:	1,950 tons
Dimensions:		$296 \times 24\frac{1}{2} \times 16$ ft
Complement:		60–70
Propulsion	surfaced:	Two diesel engines 2,400 hp
	submerged:	Two electric motors 1,600 hp
Speed	surfaced:	$15\frac{1}{2}$ knots
	submerged:	$9\frac{1}{2}$ knots
Range	surfaced:	3,800 nm at 10 knots
Armament	Gun:	Single 12 in; single 3 in AA (see armament note)
	Torpedo:	M1, M2: Four 18 in bow tubes
		M3: Four 21 in bow tubes

Class note: These boats were a development of the K Class design and have been described as submarine monitors.

Armament note: The 12 in gun had a sufficient elevation for the muzzle (on which was a foresight; the periscope acted as the backsight) to break surface with the hull awash. In this trim the weapon could be fired, but the boat had to surface for re-loading.

In *M2* the 12 in gun was removed and an aircraft hangar built in its place in front of the conning tower. A gantry was fitted to lift a small sea-plane with folding wings. *M2* sank, reportedly due to leakage of water through the hangar door, shortly after the end of the war.

M3 was converted to a minelayer with capacity for 100 mines. The 12 in gun was removed and replaced by four machine guns. Her torpedo armament was unchanged.

Losses

M1 sank after collision with SS *Vidar* off Start Point on 12 November 1926.

M2 sank as described above.

There were no war losses.

2 STEERING GEAR COMPARTMENT	11 WARD ROOM
3 MAIN ENGINE ROOM	15 FORWARD TORPEDO TUBES
4 MAIN ENGINE	16 FORWARD TORPEDO STOWAGE
5 MAIN MOTOR	17 FUEL TANKS
8 BATTERY SPACE	19 RADIO ROOM
9 CONTROL ROOM	27 W/T MAST
10 CREW ACCOMMODATION	30 3 in GUN

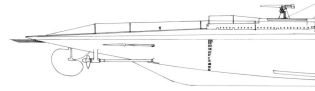

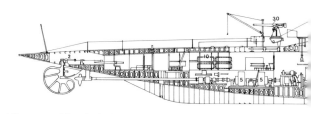

M3 converted for minelaying

M2 ready for sea and clearly showing the massive 12 in gun as well as a 3 in AA gun on a high mounting aft of the conning tower. The heavy gun mounting was later converted to an aircraft hangar.

M2 conversion for aircraft hangar.

	launched	builder
R1–R4	1918	HM Dockyard, Chatham
R7, R8	1918	Vickers
R9, R10	1918	Armstrong Whitworth
R11, R12	1918	Cammell Laird

Specification

Displacement	surfaced:	410 tons
	submerged:	500 tons
Dimensions:		$163 \times 15\frac{3}{4} \times 11\frac{1}{2}$ ft
Complement:		22
Propulsion	surfaced:	One diesel engine 240 hp
	submerged:	One electric motor 1,200 hp
Speed	surfaced:	$9\frac{1}{2}$ knots
	submerged:	15 knots
Range	surfaced:	2,000 nm at 8 knots
Armament	Torpedo:	Six 18 in bow tubes

R10 at anchor.

Class note: This was a splendid design of what would now be called a 'hunter-killer' submarine being designed to attack enemy U-Boats. But boats of this class were not completed until very late in the war and only one actually made an attack firing the full six-torpedo salvo at an enemy submarine (and missing).

The design was somewhat of a reversion to earlier practice by having internal ballast tanks and a streamlined hull. Consequently the gun was not fitted and the narrow stern allowed of only a single propeller shaft.

None of these boats was in service after 1925, all having been sold for scrap.

3 MAIN ENGINE ROOM	15 FORWARD TORPEDO TUBES
4 MAIN ENGINE	16 FORWARD TORPEDO STOWAGE
5 MAIN MOTOR	17 FUEL TANKS
8 BATTERY SPACE	20 MAIN BALLAST TANK
9 CONTROL ROOM	25 SEARCH PERISCOPE
10 CREW ACCOMMODATION	26 ATTACK PERISCOPE
11 WARD ROOM	27 W/T MAST

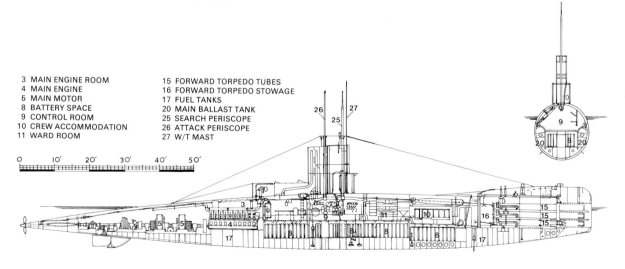

U-86 looking fully seaworthy and very modern for her time.

U-86	completed	builder
	1916	Krupp-Germania, Kiel

Specification

Displacement	surfaced:	808 tons
	submerged:	946 tons
Dimensions:		230 × 20½ ft*
Complement:		32–39
Propulsion	surfaced:	Two diesel engines 2,400 hp
	submerged:	Two electric motors 1,200 hp
Speed	surfaced:	16¾ knots
	submerged:	9 knots
Armament	Gun:	One 4.1 in; one 3.4 in
	Torpedo:	Four 19.7 in tubes; two bow, two stern

*Draught not known.

U-126 entering harbour. She is flying her number beneath the White Ensign.

U-126	completed	builder
	1918	Blohm and Voss, Hamburg

Specification

Displacement	surfaced:	1,164 tons
	submerged:	1,468 tons
Dimensions:		269 × 24½ ft*
Complement:		40
Propulsion	surfaced:	Two diesel engines 2,400 hp
	submerged:	Two electric motors 1,240 hp
Speed	surfaced:	14¾ knots
	submerged:	7¼ knots
Armament	Gun:	One or two 5.9 in
	Torpedo:	Four 19.7 in bow tubes
	Mines:	42–48 mines from two stern tubes

Note: These two submarines were commissioned into the Royal Navy under their German numbers for trials and comparisons. *U-86* was in commission from September 1919 to February 1920; *U-126* from March 1920 to September 1921. *U-86* sank in heavy weather while under tow to the breaker's yard in 1921. *U-126* was sold for breaking up in 1923.

	launched	builder
X1	1923	HM Dockyard,
		Chatham

X1 leaving harbour. The size of the two twin gun mountings can be appreciated in comparison with the height of the men on the casing.

Specification

Displacement	surfaced:	2,780 tons
	submerged:	3,600 tons
Dimensions:		350 bp × 29¾ × 15¾ ft
Complement:		110
Propulsion	surfaced:	Diesel engines 6,000 hp
	submerged:	Electric motors 2,600 hp
Armament	Gun:	Four 5.2 in two twin mountings with cupola-type shields; two twin mg (AA)
	Torpedo:	Six 21 in bow tubes
Speed	surfaced:	19½ knots
	submerged:	9 knots
Range	surfaced:	12,500 nm at 12 knots

Note: This design evolved from intelligence gained from the World War I Cruiser submarines of the German Navy. *X1* was produced very largely as an experiment and the gun armament was at the limit permitted in the Naval Defence Act. The boat suffered from numerous malfunctions in service; after five years she was laid up, and was scrapped in 1936. The bow of *X1* retained the shape or profile similar to the K Class boats of World War I.

Osiris entering Portsmouth harbour. The radio aerials were high, as can be seen by the angle of the insulators. This Class had quite high freeboard when trimmed for surface running.

Group 1

	launched	builder
O1 (later *Oberon*)	1926	HM Dockyard, Chatham
OA2 (later *Otway*), *OA1* (later *Oxley*)	1926	Vickers Armstrong

Specification

Displacement	surfaced:	1,350 tons (*O1* 1,311 tons)
	submerged:	1,870 tons (*O1* 1,831 tons)
Dimensions:		275 bp × 27¾ × 13¼ ft
		(*O1* 270 bp × 28 × 13¼ ft)
Complement:		54
Propulsion	surfaced:	Diesel engines 3,000 bhp
	submerged:	Electric motors 1,350 bhp
		Two shafts
Speed	surfaced:	*O1* 17½ knots
	submerged:	*OA1, OA2* 15½ knots
Range	surfaced:	8,500 nm at 10 knots
Armament	Gun:	Single 4 in; two mg (AA)
	Torpedo:	Eight 21 in tubes; six bow, two stern

Group 2

	launched	builder
Odin	1928	HM Dockyard, Chatham
Olympus	1928	Beardmore
Orpheus	1929	Beardmore
Osiris, Oswald, Otus	1928	Vickers Armstrong, Barrow-in-Furness

Specification

Displacement	surfaced:	1,475 tons
	submerged:	2,030 tons
Dimensions:		260 bp × 29¾ × 13¾ ft
Complement:		53
Propulsion	surfaced:	Diesel engines 4,400 hp
	submerged:	Electric motors 1,325 hp
		Two shafts
		Fuel capacity 200 tons

Speed and Range as Group 1
Armament as Group 1

Class note: This Class was the leading design of post-World War I submarines for the Royal Navy. There were many teething troubles, and new features were introduced. Strengthened pressure hulls were used and fuel was carried in the ballast tanks which aided rapid diving but tanks were of light construction and fuel leakage was experienced. The boats had an extended surface range. Forty-four ft periscopes were fitted and Asdic equipment.

With the exception of Nautilus and Swordfish (c. 1915–16) this Class were the first boats to be named.

OA2 and OA1 were built for the Royal Australian Navy but were transferred to the Royal Navy in 1931.

Armament note: Oberon, designed in 1924, was intended to have either a 4 in or a 4.7 in gun with Lewis guns for AA protection.

Losses

Oxley was mistaken for a U-Boat and rammed by HM S/M Triton on 10 September 1939 off the coast of Norway. This was the first British naval loss in World War II.

Odin was sunk by gunfire from the Italian destroyer Strale in the Gulf of Taranto on 14 June 1940.

Olympus was mined and sank off Malta on 8 May 1942.

Orpheus was depth-charged by the Italian destroyer Turbine in the eastern Mediterranean on 27 June 1940.

Oswald was rammed by the Italian destroyer Vivaldi south of Calabria on 1 August 1940.

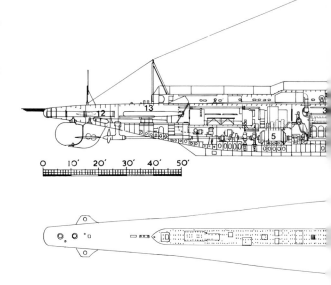

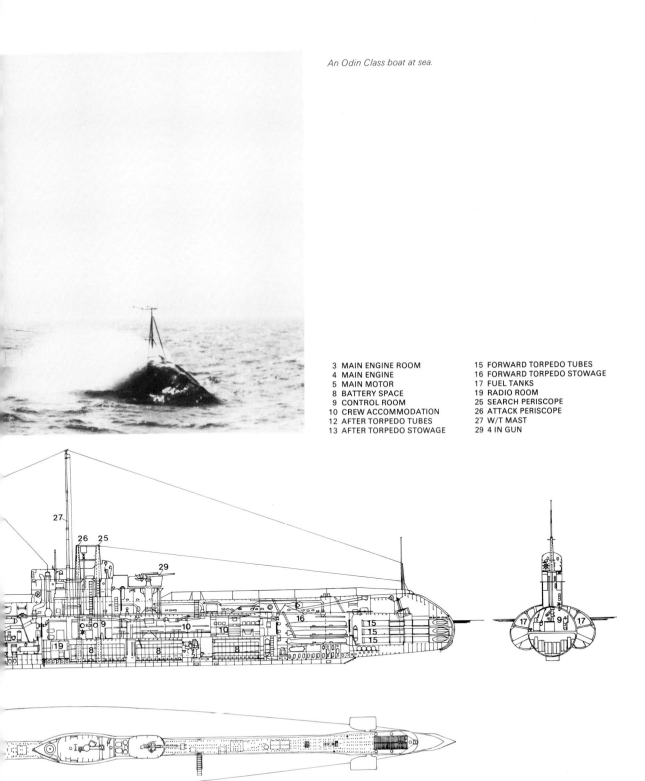

An Odin Class boat at sea.

3 MAIN ENGINE ROOM
4 MAIN ENGINE
5 MAIN MOTOR
8 BATTERY SPACE
9 CONTROL ROOM
10 CREW ACCOMMODATION
12 AFTER TORPEDO TUBES
13 AFTER TORPEDO STOWAGE

15 FORWARD TORPEDO TUBES
16 FORWARD TORPEDO STOWAGE
17 FUEL TANKS
19 RADIO ROOM
25 SEARCH PERISCOPE
26 ATTACK PERISCOPE
27 W/T MAST
29 4 IN GUN

Proteus exercising at sea with her 4 in gun elevated and trained to starboard.

	launched	builder
Parthion	1929	HM Dockyard, Chatham
Perseus	1929	Vickers Armstrong
Phoenix	1929	Cammell Laird
Poseidon	1929	Vickers Armstrong
Proteus	1929	Vickers Armstrong
Pandora (ex *Python*)	1929	Vickers Armstrong

Specification

Displacement	surfaced:	1,760 tons
	submerged:	2,040 tons
Dimensions:		$289 \times 28 \times 13\frac{1}{2}$ ft
Complement:		56
Propulsion	surfaced:	Two diesel engines, 4,400 hp
	submerged:	Two electric motors, 1,350 hp
		Two shafts
Armament	Gun:	One 4 in
	Torpedo:	Eight 21 in tubes, six bow and two stern
Speed	surfaced:	18 knots
	submerged:	9 knots
Range:		8,500 nm at 10 knots

Class note: These boats had a higher surface speed than the previous O Class.

Gun armament note: *Perseus* had one 4.7 in gun on commissioning, and had this replaced temporarily with an experimental 4.9 in gun.

Losses

Parthion struck a mine and sank on 11 August 1943 in the southern Adriatic.

Perseus whilst off Zante, was sighted on 1 December 1941 and torpedoed by the Italian submarine *Enrico Toti*.

Phoenix was a contact of the Italian TB *Albatross* and was depth charged and lost off Sicily on 17 July 1940.

Pandora was bombed and sank by Italian aircraft in Valetta Dockyard on 1 April 1942.

Poseidon sank in collision with SS *Yuta* off Wei-Hai-Wei in the Gulf of Korea on 9 June 1931.

Pandora with the forward hydroplanes folded flush with the hull and the torpedo davit apparently ready for use.

	launched	builder
Rainbow	1930	HM Dockyard, Chatham
Regent, Regulus, Rover	1930	Vickers Armstrong
Cancellations:		*Royalist* (Beardmore) and *Rupert* (Cammell Laird) were cancelled in 1929.

Specification

Displacement	surfaced:	1,740 tons
	submerged:	2,015 tons
Dimensions:		$287 \times 28 \times 13\frac{1}{2}$ ft
Complement:		51
Propulsion	surfaced:	Two diesel engines 4,400 hp
	submerged:	Two electric motors 1,320 hp
Armament	Gun:	Single 4 in (see armament note)
	Torpedo:	Eight 21 in tubes; six bow, two stern
Speed	surfaced:	$17\frac{1}{2}$ knots
	submerged:	9 knots

Rover at speed with a crowded conning tower. This is an early design of the 'conventional' submarine.

Class note: This was the first Class to include a bathroom for those lodged in the Ward Room, but the fresh water capacity was not increased.

Armament note: As designed a 4.7 in gun was mounted, but later replaced by a 4 in gun.

Losses

Rainbow was torpedoed by the Italian submarine *Enrico Toti* off Calabria on or about 19 October 1940.
Regent was mined in the Strait of Otranto on 16 April 1943.
Regulus was lost, cause unknown, in the Strait of Otranto on 6 December 1940.

Severn on builder's trials.

	launched	builder
Thames	1932	Vickers Armstrong
Clyde, Severn	1934	Vickers Armstrong

Specification

Displacement	surfaced:	2,165 tons
	submerged:	2,680 tons
Dimensions:		245 × 28 × 13½ ft
Complement:		61
Propulsion	surfaced:	Two diesel engines 10,000 hp
	submerged:	Two electric motors, 2,500 hp
Speed	surfaced:	22½ knots
	submerged:	10 knots
Range	surfaced:	12,000 nm at 8 knots
Armament	Gun:	Single 4 in
	Torpedo:	Six 21 in bow tubes

Class note: Yet again an attempt to return, albeit with conventional propulsion methods, to the Fleet Submarine similar to the K class of World War I. These boats were quite large and, it is understood, very comfortable. They were designed with a somewhat light armament for their tonnage.

Armament note: *Thames* was first fitted with one 4.7 in gun which was later replaced with a 4 in gun.

Loss
Thames struck a mine and sank off Norway on 23 July 1940.

Group 1	launched	builder
Sturgeon, Seahorse	1932	HM Dockyard, Chatham
Swordfish	1931	HM Dockyard, Chatham
Starfish	1933	HM Dockyard, Chatham

Specification

Displacement	surfaced:	735 tons
	submerged:	935 tons
Dimensions:		202½ × 24 × 12 ft
Complement:		36
Propulsion	surfaced:	Two 8 cyl diesel engines 1,550 hp
	submerged:	Two electric motors 1,300 hp
		Fuel capacity 40 tons
Speed	surfaced:	14 knots
	submerged:	10 knots
Range	surfaced:	3,750 nm at 10 knots
Armament	Gun:	Single 3 in
	Torpedo:	Six 21 in bow tubes

Group 2	launched	builder
Sealion, Salmon	1934	Cammell Laird
Shark, Snapper	1934	HM Dockyard, Chatham
Seawolf	1935	Scotts
Spearfish	1936	Cammell Laird
Sunfish	1936	HM Dockyard, Chatham
Sterlet	1937	HM Dockyard, Chatham

Specification as Group 1 except:

Displacement	surfaced:	765 tons
	submerged:	960 tons
Dimensions:		length increased to 208 ft
Diving depth:		rivetted hull boats 300 ft
		welded hull boats 350 ft

Sickle after leaving the builder's yard on the Mersey. The direction finding aerial is mounted on the casing behind the 'bandstand' aft of the conning tower.

Group 3

	launched	builder
P61 (later *P211, Safari*)	1941	Cammell Laird
P62 (later *P212, Sahib*) *P63* (later *P213, Saracen*)	1942	Cammell Laird
P64 (later *P214, Satyr*)	1942	Scotts
P65 (later *P215, Sceptre*)	1943	Scotts
P66 (later *P216, Seadog*) *P67* (later *P217, Sibyl*)	1942	Cammell Laird
P68 (later *P218, Sea Rover*)	1943	Scotts (completed by Vickers Armstrong)
P69 (later *P219, Seraph*), *P71* (later *P221, Shakespeare*), *P72* (later *P222*)	1941	Vickers Armstrong
P223 (later *Sea Nymph*), *P224* (later *Sickle*), *P225* (later *Simoom*)	1942	Cammell Laird
P226 (later *Sirdar*)	1943	Scotts (completed by Vickers Armstrong)
P227 (later *Spiteful*)	1943	Scotts
P228 (later *Splendid*),	1942	HM Dockyard, Chatham
P229 (later *Sportsman*)	1942	HM Dockyard, Chatham
P231 (later *Stoic*), *P232* (later *Stonehenge*), *P233* (later *Storm*), *P234* (later *Stratagem*)	1943	Cammell Laird
P235 (later *Strongbow*), *P236* (later *Spark*)	1943	Scotts
P237 (later *Scythian*)	1944	Scots
P238 (later *Stubborn*), *P239* (later *Surf*)	1942	Cammell Laird
Syrtis, Spirit, Statesman, Sturdy, Stygian, Shalimar	1943	Cammell Laird HM Dockyard, Chatham
Scotsman	1944	Scotts
Sea Devil	1945	Scotts
Subtle, Supreme, Sea Scout, Selene, Scorcher, Sidon, Sleuth, Solent	1944	Cammell Laird

S CLASS (continued)

	launched	builder
Spearhead, Spur	1944	Cammell Laird
Seneschal, Sentinel	1945	Scotts
Saga, Springer, Sanguine	1945	Cammell Laird

Cancellations: The following, under construction with Cammell Laird, were cancelled or broken up: *Sea Robin, Spritely, Surface* and *Surge*. The number *P230* was not allocated.

Specification similar to Group 1, and diving capability as Group 2, except:

Displacement	surfaced:	814 tons
	submerged:	990 tons
Dimensions:		$217 \times 24 \times 13\frac{1}{4}$ ft
Armament	Gun:	Some boats mounted a 4 in in lieu of the 3 in gun
	Torpedo:	Seven 21 in tubes; six bow, one stern

(Class note, Armament note and Losses are on page 66.)

2 STEERING GEAR COMPARTMENT
3 MAIN ENGINE ROOM
4 MAIN ENGINE
5 MAIN MOTOR
8 BATTERY SPACE
9 CONTROL ROOM
10 CREW ACCOMMODATION
11 WARD ROOM
12 AFTER TORPEDO TUBES
15 FORWARD TORPEDO TUBES
16 FORWARD TORPEDO STOWAGE
17 FUEL TANKS
19 RADIO ROOM
23 'Q' TANK
25 SEARCH PERISCOPE
26 ATTACK PERISCOPE
27 W/T MAST
28 RADAR MAST
30 3 in GUN

GROUP 1

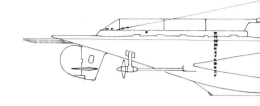

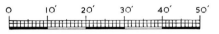

GROUP 2

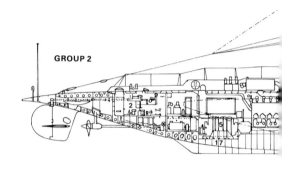

GROUP 3

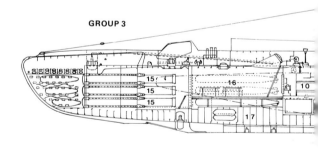

GROUP 3 MODIFIED, 1953

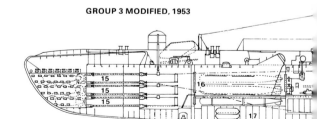

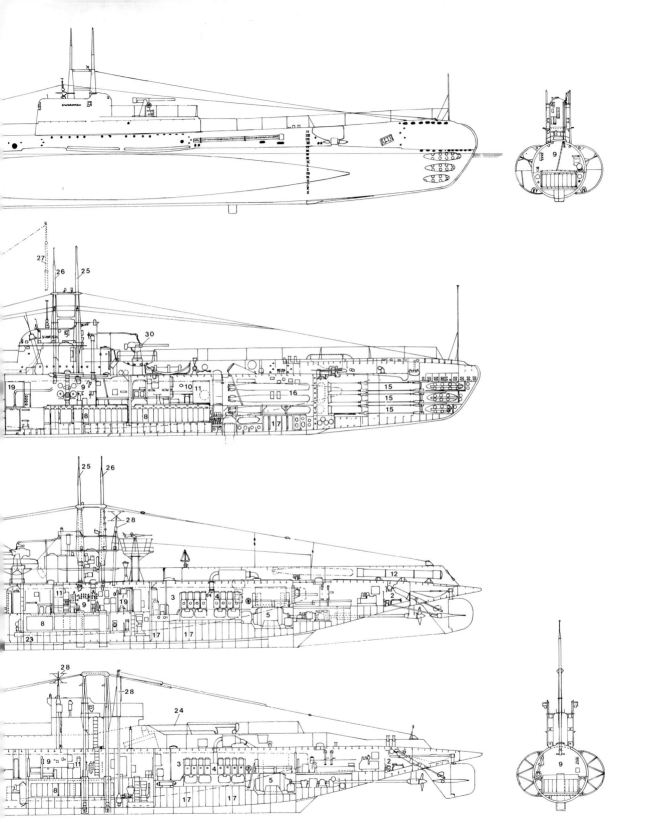

S CLASS (continued)

Class note: This Class totalled 62 boats commissioned. The design was influenced by the Admiralty decision to standardise on a short-range and a long-range Class: this was the short-range Class and T Class (see p. 74) was to fulfil the long-range role.

(see p. 74)

Group 1 were all completed by the end of 1933; mines could be carried in lieu of torpedoes. The first boat in Group 3 was numbered *P211*. Later the Prime Minister, Winston Churchill, decided that all submarines would be named. However, names were not allocated immediately to *P226* and *P230*; *Sirdar* was the first to be launched under her name rather than number.

Armament note: In Group 1 *Sturgeon* and *Swordfish* had a 3 in DP/HA disappearing gun; later boats in this group had a 3 in fixed gun. The boats in Group 3 carrying a 4 in gun required an increase in complement of three.

Losses

Sahib was depth-charged by the Italian escort vessel *Gabbiano* on 24 April 1943, and was abandoned and scuttled off the north coast of Sicily.

Salmon was mined in Norwegian waters on 9 July 1940.

Saracen was depth-charged and sunk by the Italian corvette *Minerva* off Bastia on 18 August 1943.

Seahorse was sunk by the German First Minesweeping flotilla in the Heligoland Bight on 7 January 1940.

Shark was sunk by German minesweepers *M1803*, *M1806* and *M1807* off Skudesneshavn, Norway, on 6 July 1940.

Sickle is believed to have been mined in the Antikitheria Channel in the eastern Mediterranean on or about 18 June 1944.

Simoom was assumed lost, cause unknown, in the Dardanelles on 19 November 1943.

Snapper was assumed lost in the Bay of Biscay, cause unknown, on 12 February 1942.

Spearfish was torpedoed by *U-34* off the coast of Norway sometime before 5 August 1940.

Splendid was sunk by the German destroyer *Hermes** off the west coast of Corsica on 21 April 1943.

Starfish was depth-charged and sunk by the German minesweeper *M7* in the Heligoland Bight on 9 January 1940.

Sterlet was depth-charged by the German anti-submarine trawlers *UJ125*, *UJ126* and *UJ127* in the Skaggerak on 18 April 1940.

Stonehenge was lost, cause unknown, off the Nicobar Islands on or about 22 March 1944.

Stratagem was depth-charged and sunk by a Japanese patrol craft off Malacca on 22 November 1943.

Swordfish was lost, cause unknown, off Ushant on or about 16 November 1940.

Syrtis was mined off Bodö, Norway, on 28 March 1944.

P222 was sunk by the Italian TB *Fortunale* off Naples on 12 December 1942.

Simoom in an almost identical situation to Sickle. Simoom has the high HF/DF aerial on the conning tower in addition to the DF type on the after casing.

Sportsman sank off Toulon on 24 September 1952 while on loan to the French Navy.

Sidon was wrecked by an accidental torpedo explosion in Portland dockyard on 16 May 1955.

Sunfish was sunk in error by Allied aircraft on 27 July 1944. She was on passage to Murmansk for transfer to the Russian Navy as *B1*.

*Hermes had been taken over from the Greek Navy, in which she was named *Vasilevs Georgios*.

Testing the torpedo tube of an S Class submarine.

	launched	builder
Grampus	1936	HM Dockyard, Chatham
Porpoise	1932	Vickers Armstrong, Barrow-in-Furness
Narwhal	1935	Vickers Armstrong, Barrow-in-Furness
Rorqual	1936	Vickers Armstrong, Barrow-in-Furness
Cachalot	1937	Scotts
Seal	1938	HM Dockyard, Chatham
Cancellations:		*P411*, *P412* and *P413*, all with Scotts, were cancelled in 1941

Specification

Displacement	surfaced:	1,520 tons (*Porpoise* 1,500 tons)
	submerged:	2,157 tons (*Porpoise* 2,055 tons)
Dimensions:		$289 \times 25\frac{1}{2} \times 15\frac{1}{2}$ ft
		(*Porpoise* $288 \times 30 \times 14$ ft)
Complement:		59
Propulsion	surfaced:	Two diesel engines 3,300 bhp
	submerged:	Two electric motors 1,630 bhp
Speed	surfaced:	15 knots
	submerged:	9 knots
Range	surfaced:	7,500 nm at 10 knots
Armament	Gun:	Single 4 in
	Torpedo:	Six 21 in bow tubes
	Mines:	50

Class note: The Class was intended to succeed the M Class. The periscope standards were offset vertically to starboard within the inner conning tower to allow a clear run for the mine-carrying railway which ran down the centre line from the inner bow to the outer stern doors. Compensating ballast was carried on the port side to ensure stability.

Losses

Cachalot was rammed by an Italian TB off Cyrenaica on 4 August 1941.

Grampus was depth-charged by the Italian TBs *Circe* and *Clio* off Augusta on 24 June 1940.

Narwhal was lost, cause unknown, off the Norwegian coast on or about 1 August 1940.

Porpoise was bombed by Japanese aircraft in the Malacca Strait on 19 January 1945. She was the last Royal Navy submarine to be lost in World War II.

Seal was captured in the Kattegat on 5 May 1940. She was spotted by German aircraft and, the water being too shallow to allow a full dive, her Captain and crew abandoned her. They were taken prisoner and the Germans had a splendid gift, which they evaluated and commissioned as *U-4*.

2 STEERING GEAR COMPARTMENT	15 FORWARD TORPEDO TUBES
3 MAIN ENGINE ROOM	16 FORWARD TORPEDO STOWAGE
4 MAIN ENGINE	19 RADIO ROOM
5 MAIN MOTOR	25 SEARCH PERISCOPE
8 BATTERY SPACE	26 ATTACK PERISCOPE
9 CONTROL ROOM	27 W/T MAST
10 CREW ACCOMMODATION	29 4 in GUN
11 WARD ROOM	

Narwhal on the surface at speed.

Usk on builder's trials.

Group 1

	launched	builder
Undine	1937	Vickers Armstrong, Barrow-in-Furness
Unity, Ursula	1938	Vickers Armstrong, Barrow-in-Furness
Umpire (ex *P31*)*	1940	HM Dockyard, Chatham
Una (ex *P32*)	1941	HM Dockyard, Chatham
Unbeaten (ex *P33*), *Undaunted* (ex *P34*), *Union* (ex *P35*), *Unique* (ex *P36*), *Upholder* (ex *P37*), *Upright* (ex *P38*), *Urchin* (ex *P39*), *Urge* (ex *P40*), *Usk* (ex *P41*), *Utmost* (ex *P42*)	1940	Vickers Armstrong, Barrow-in-Furness

*Each of the Class from *Umpire* onwards had the name changed to a number and later reverted to the original name.

Specification

Displacement	surfaced:	540 tons
	submerged:	730 tons
Dimensions:		$191\frac{1}{2} \times 16 \times 12\frac{3}{4}$ ft (*Umpire, Una, Unbeaten, Undaunted, Union, Urchin, Urge* and *Usk* were $196\frac{3}{4}$ ft long; beam and draft unchanged)
Complement:		31 (except *Undine, Unity,* and *Ursula*: 27)
Propulsion	surfaced:	Two diesel engines 615 bhp
	submerged:	Two electric motors 825 bhp Fuel capacity 41 tons
Speed	surfaced:	$11\frac{3}{4}$ knots
	submerged:	9 knots
Range	surfaced:	4,100 nm at 10 knots

Diving depth:		Group 1 and 2, 200 ft
Armament	Gun:	Single 3 in or 12 pdr (except *Undine* and *Unity*)
	Torpedo:	Six 21 in bow tubes, four internal, 2 external (*Umpire, Una, Unbeaten, Undaunted, Union, Urchin, Urge* and *Usk* had four 21 in bow tubes only)

Group 2

	launched	builder
P31(II) (ex *Ullswater*, later *Uproar*), *P32*	1940	Vickers Armstrong, Barrow-in-Furness
P33, P34(II) (later *Ultimatum*), *P35(II)* (later *Umbra*), *P36, P37(II)* (later *Unbending*), *P38, P39, P41(II), P42(II)* (later *Unbroken*), *P43* (later *Unison*), *P44* (later *United*), *P46* (later *Unruffled*)	1941	Vickers Armstrong, Barrow-in-Furness
P45 (later *Unrivalled*), *P47, P48, P49* (later *Unruly*), *P51* (later *Unseen*), *P52, P53* (later *Ultor*), *P54* (later *Unshaken*)	1942	Vickers Armstrong, Barrow-in-Furness
P55 (later *Unsparing*), *P56* (later *Usurper*), *P57* (later *Universal*), *P58* (later *Untamed*), *P59* (later *Untiring*)	1942	Vickers Armstrong, Newcastle upon Tyne

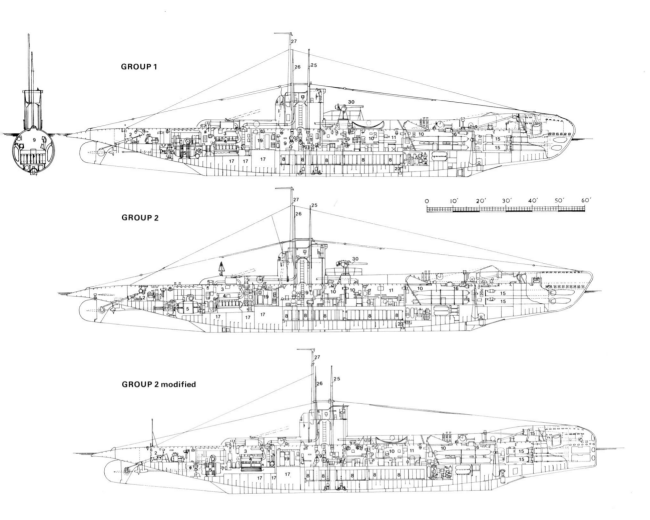

GROUP 1

GROUP 2

GROUP 2 modified

	launched	builder
P61 (later *Varangian*), P62 (later *Uther*), P63 (later *Unswerving*)	1943	Vickers Armstrong, Newcastle upon Tyne
P64 (later *Vandal*), P65 (later *Upstart*)	1942	Vickers Armstrong, Barrow-in-Furness
P66 (later *Varne I*), P67 (later *Vox I*)	1943	Vickers Armstrong, Barrow-in-Furness

2 STEERING GEAR COMPARTMENT
3 MAIN ENGINE ROOM
4 MAIN ENGINE
5 MAIN MOTOR
8 BATTERY SPACE
9 CONTROL ROOM
10 CREW ACCOMMODATION
11 WARD ROOM
15 FORWARD TORPEDO TUBES

16 FORWARD TORPEDO STOWAGE
17 FUEL TANKS
19 RADIO ROOM
23 'Q' TANK
25 SEARCH PERISCOPE
26 ATTACK PERISCOPE
27 W/T MAST
30 3 in GUN

Specification as Group 1 except:
Displacement surfaced: 545 tons
submerged: 740 tons
Dimensions: This Group was 197 ft long; beam and draught as Group 1
Armament Gun: Single 3 in and three machine guns
Torpedo: Four 21 in bow tubes

Cancellations: *P81–P87, Veto, Virile, Visitant, Upas, Ulex, Utopia* (Vickers Armstrong, Barrow-in-Furness); *Unbridled, Upward, Vantage, Vehement, Venom, Verve* and a further eight unnamed (Vickers Armstrong, Newcastle upon Tyne)

U CLASS (continued)

Class note: The Class was initially designed for training purposes, without armament which was fitted later. They were very small but handy boats of single hull construction with internal fuel and ballast compartments.

Losses

Undine was depth-charged by German minesweepers *M1201*, *M1204* and *M1207* in the Heligoland Bight on 7 January 1940.

Unity sank in a surface collision with SS *Atle Jarl* off the River Tyne on 29 April 1940.

Umpire was mistaken for a U-boat by the anti-submarine trawler *Peter Hendriks* off the Wash and rammed on 19 July 1941.

Unbeaten was mistaken for a U-boat in the Bay of Biscay and bombed by the RAF on 11 November 1942.

Undaunted was lost, cause unknown, off Tripoli on 13 May 1941.

Union was sunk by Italian patrol craft off the Tunisian coast on 22 July 1941.

Unique was lost, cause unknown, to the west of Gibraltar on 24 October 1942.

Upholder was depth-charged by the Italian TB *Pegaso* off Tripoli on 14 April 1942.

Urge was depth-charged by the Italian TB *Pegaso* off Tripoli on 28 April 1942.

Usk was mined and sank off Cape Bon on 3 May 1941.

Utmost was depth-charged by the Italian TB *Groppo* off the west coast of Sicily on 24 November 1942.

P32 was mined off Tripoli on 18 August 1941.

P33 is believed to have been mined off Tripoli on 20 August 1941.

P36 was bombed by Italian aircraft in Sliema Creek, Valetta, on 1 April 1942.

P38 was depth-charged by the Italian TB *Circe* and *Usodimare* off the Tunisian coast on 25 February 1942.

U Class boat at sea.

P39 was bombed in Valetta harbour on 26 March 1942.

P41 was lost, cause unknown, in the Bodö area off the Norwegian coast on or about 24 February 1943. She was at that time in the Royal Netherlands Navy with the name *Uredd*.

P48 was depth-charged by the Italian corvette *Ardente* in the Gulf of Tunis on 25 December 1942.

P56 was depth-charged by the German patrol boat *UJ-2208* in the Gulf of Genoa on 11 October 1943.

P58 was lost in an accident in the Clyde submarine exercise area on 30 May 1943. She was salvaged and re-commissioned as *Vitality*.

Vandal foundered in the Firth of Clyde on 24 February 1943.

Venturer in the Clyde exercise area.

	launched	builder
Upshot, Variance, Vengeful, Vineyard	1944	Vickers Armstrong, Barrow-in-Furness
Urtica, Vagabond, Varne (II), Virulent, Volatile, Vortex, Votary	1944	Vickers Armstong, Newcastle upon Tyne
Vampire, Vivid, Voracious, Vulpine	1943	Vickers Armstrong, Newcastle upon Tyne
Veldt, Venturer, Vigorous, Viking, Virtue, Visigoth, Vox (II)	1943	Vickers Armstrong, Barrow-in-Furness

Cancellations: *Ulex, Unbridled, Upas, Upward, Utopia, Vantage, Vehement, Venom, Verve, Veto, Virile, Visitant* (Vickers Armstrong at either Tyne or Barrow).

Specification

Displacement	surfaced:	545 tons
	submerged:	740 tons
Dimensions:		$204\frac{1}{2} \times 16 \times 12\frac{3}{4}$ ft
Complement:		37
Propulsion	surfaced:	Two diesel engines 800 bhp
	submerged:	Two electric motors 760 bhp
Speed	surfaced:	13 knots
	submerged:	9 knots
Range	surfaced:	4,050 nm at 10 knots
	Diving	
	depth:	300 ft
Armament	Gun:	Single 3 in
	Torpedo:	Four 21 in bow tubes

Class note: The U and V Classes were very largely comprised of boats of the same design (similar to the V and W Classes of destroyers in World War I) and were arbitrarily split into two named groups.

Upshot leaving Barrow. She has the DF aerial mounted on the pressure hull.

Teredo at sea. The aft-firing tubes on the casing are noticeable as are the tubes in the bow and stern casing.

Group 1

	launched	builder
Triton	1937	Vickers Armstrong, Barrow-in-Furness
Thetis (later *Thunderbolt*),		
Trident	1938	Cammell Laird
Tribune	1938	Scotts
Triumph, Thistle	1938	Vickers Armstrong, Barrow-in-Furness
Taku	1939	Cammell Laird
Tarpon	1939	Scotts
Tigris	1939	HM Dockyard, Chatham
Triad, Truant, Tetrarch	1939	Vickers Armstrong, Barrow-in-Furness
Tuna	1940	Scotts
Talisman, Thrasher	1940	Cammell Laird
Torbay	1940	HM Dockyard, Chatham
Tempest, Thorn	1941	Cammell Laird
Traveller	1941	Scotts
Trusty, Turbulent	1941	Vickers Armstrong, Barrow-in-Furness
Trooper	1942	Scotts

Specification

Displacement	surfaced:	1325 tons (*Triton* 1,095 tons)
	submerged:	1,580 (*Triton* 1,579 tons)
Dimensions:		274 × 26½ × 16¼ ft
Complement:		59

Propulsion	surfaced:	Two diesel engines 2,500 hp
	submerged:	Two electric motors, 1,450 hp
		Two shafts
		Fuel capacity 210 tons
Speed	surfaced:	15¼ knots
	submerged:	9 knots
Range	surfaced:	9,510 nm
Diving depth:		Rivetted hull boats 300 ft
		Welded hull boats 350 ft
Armament	Gun:	Single 4 in
	Torpedo:	Ten 21 in tubes, six internal and two external at the bow; one tube on each beam (see armament note)

	launched	builder
Group 2		
P91 (ex *Tutankhamen*, later *P311*), *Tactician* (ex *P94*, later *P314*), *Taurus* (ex *P93*, *P313*, later *P339*), *Templar* (ex *P96*, later *P316*)	1942	Vickers Armstrong, Barrow-in-Furness
P325 (later *Thule*)	1942	HM Dockyard, Devonport
P327 (later *Tireless*), *P328* (later *Token*)	1943	HM Dockyard, Portsmouth
P92 (ex *P312*, later *Trespasser*), *P95* (ex *P315*, later *Truculent*)	1942	Vickers Armstrong, Barrow-in-Furness
P326 (later *Tudor*)	1942	HM Dockyard, Devonport
P322 (later *Talent (I)*), *P99* (ex *P319*, later *Tantivy*)	1943	Vickers Armstrong, Barrow-in-Furness, completed by Clydebank
P97 (ex *P317*, later *Tally-Ho*)	1942	Vickers Armstrong, Barrow-in-Furness, completed by Clydebank

	launched	builder
P98 (ex *P318*, later *Tantalus*), *P321* (later *Telemachus*), *P324* (later *Thorough*)	1943	Vickers Armstrong, Barrow-in-Furness
P323 (later *Terrapin*)	1943	Vickers Armstrong, Barrow-in-Furness, completed by Bellis & Morcom
Tiptoe, Trump, Tapir	1944	Vickers Armstrong, Barrow-in-Furness, completed by Clydebank
Totem	1943	HM Dockyard, Devonport
P329 (later *Tradewind*)	1942	HM Dockyard, Chatham
Trenchant	1943	HM Dockyard, Chatham
Taciturn	1944	Vickers Armstrong, Barrow-in-Furness, completed by Bellis & Morcom
Tabard	1945	Scotts
Truncheon	1944	HM Dockyard, Devonport
Turpin	1944	HM Dockyard, Chatham
Tarn	1944	Vickers Armstrong, Barrow-in-Furness

T CLASS (continued)

	launched	builder
Tasman (later *Talent III*)	1945	Vickers Armstrong, Barrow-in-Furness, completed by Bellis & Morcom
Teredo	1945	Vickers Armstrong, Barrow-in-Furness, completed by Clydebank
Thermopylae	1945	HM Dockyard, Chatham
Cancellations:		*Talent II* (Scotts); *Theban, Threat* (Vickers Armstrong, Barrow-in-Furness); *Thor, Tiara* (HM Dockyard, Portsmouth). *Typhoon* was projected but not ordered

Specification

Displacement	surfaced:	1,090 tons
	submerged:	1,575 tons
Dimensions:		$275 \times 26\frac{1}{2} \times 14\frac{3}{4}$ ft
Complement:		65
Propulsion and speed		as Group 1
Range:		11,000 nm at 10 knots
Diving	depth:	as Group 1
Armament:	Gun:	Single 4 in, single 20 mm, three mg
	Torpedo:	Eleven 21 in tubes: six internal and two external at the bow; two mounted externally on either beam aft of the conning tower, firing aft; one external at the stern

GROUP 1, 1938

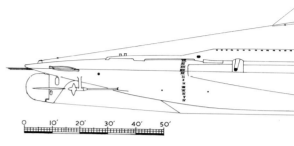

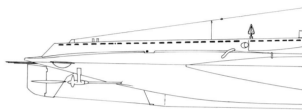

GROUP 3, 1946

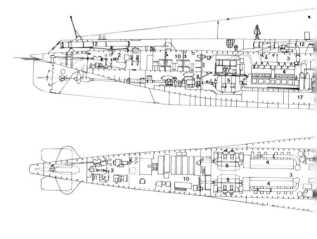

Tireless and Alaric moored at Trafford Wharf, Manchester, for the Queen's Coronation, 1953. Note the differences in their sterns.

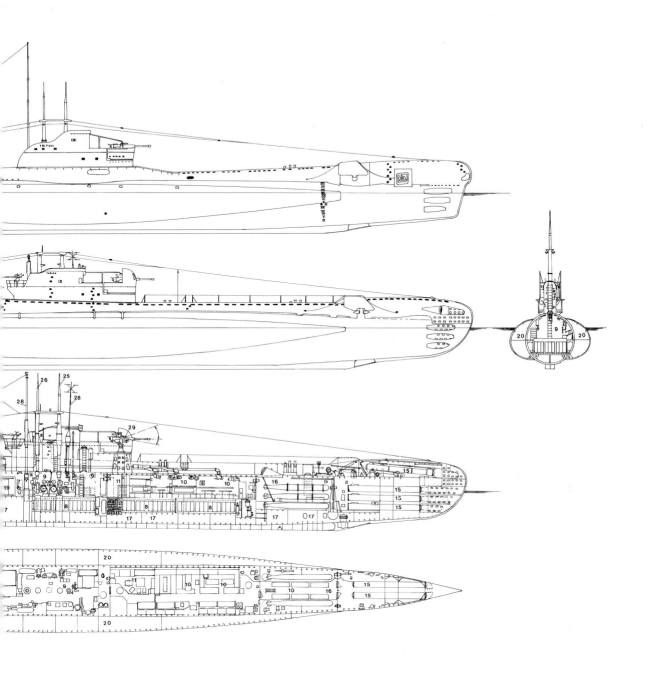

2 STEERING GEAR COMPARTMENT	15 FORWARD TORPEDO TUBES
3 MAIN ENGINE ROOM	16 FORWARD TORPEDO STOWAGE
4 MAIN ENGINE	17 FUEL TANKS
5 MAIN MOTOR	19 RADIO ROOM
8 BATTERY SPACE	20 MAIN BALLAST TANK
9 CONTROL ROOM	25 SEARCH PERISCOPE
10 CREW ACCOMMODATION	26 ATTACK PERISCOPE
11 WARD ROOM	28 RADAR MAST
12 TORPEDO TUBES	29 4 in GUN

T CLASS (continued)

Class note: This Class was the first to be fitted with Radar and, later, Snorkel equipment.

Armament note: This Class gave the guns a steadier firing platform for surface action. In Group 1 a salvo of ten torpedoes was available for firing forward: the two beam tubes (just aft of the conning tower) were angled outwards to clear the forward hydroplanes.

The external tubes could not be reloaded until the boat returned to harbour.

Losses

Talisman was lost, cause unknown, on or before 18 September 1942 in the Sicilian Channel.

Tarpon was sunk by the German minesweeper *M6* in the North Sea on 14 April 1940.

Triton was sunk by the Itlain TB *Clio* in the Adriatic Sea on 8 December 1940.

Tempest was depth-charged by the Italian TB *Circe* in the Gulf of Taranto on 13 February 1942.

Tetrarch was lost, cause unknown, in the western Mediterranean on or about 2 November 1941.

Thistle was torpedoed by *U-4* off Skudesneshavn, Norway, on 10 April 1940.

Thorn was depth-charged by the Italian TB *Pegaso* off Torbruk on 6 August 1942.

Tigris was lost, cause unknown, on or about 10 March 1943 in the Gulf of Naples.

Traveller was lost, cause unknown, in the Gulf of Taranto on or about 12 December 1942.

Triad was lost, cause unknown, off the coast of Libya on or about 20 October 1940.

Triumph was lost, cause unknown, in the Aegean Sea on or about 14 January 1942.

Trooper was lost, possibly mined, in the Aegean Sea on or about 17 October 1943.

Turbulent was depth-charged by an Italian MA/SB off the coast of Sardinia on or about 23 March 1943.

Thetis foundered while on trial in Liverpool Bay on 1 June 1939. After some successful dives she failed to surface and the escort vessel reported the then equivalent of 'subsunk'. Salvage vessels arrived late on the scene and *Thetis's* stern broke surface for long enough for a hole to be cut in the hull. Only two men were rescued and the air grew foul in the submarine. Despite the salvage vessels and destroyer flotilla on the surface she could not be saved.

She was salvaged and re-commissioned as *Thunderbolt*.

Thunderbolt was depth-charged by the Italian MA/SB *Cicogna* north of Sicily on 13 March 1943.

P311 was mined and sank north of Corsica on or about 8 January 1943.

Terrapin survived a depth-charge attack in the Pacific by Japanese surface craft on 19 May 1945, but was declared a constructive loss on her return to harbour.

Truculent sank after collision with the MV *Dvina* in the Medway estuary on 12 January 1950.

The conning tower of Tally-Ho. The AA gun has been removed from the 'bandstand'.

Tally-Ho from the air.

One of the ex-US Navy R Class. Note the silhouette of the gun by comparison with the British 3 or 4 in piece.

	launched	builder
P511 (ex R3)	1919	Fore River
P512 (ex R17)	1917	Union Iron Works
P514 (ex R19)	1918	Union Iron Works

Specification

Displacement	surfaced:	569 tons
	submerged:	680 tons
Dimensions:		179 wl × 18¼ × 14½ ft
Complement:		33
Propulsion	surfaced:	Two diesel engines 880 bhp
	submerged:	Two electric motors 934 bhp
Speed	surfaced:	13½ knots
	submerged:	10½ knots
Armament	Gun:	Single 3 in
	Torpedo:	Four 21 in bow tubes

Class note: On a similar principle to the 'Destroyers for Bases' agreement between the US and UK governments, nine submarines (this and the S Class), albeit rather ancient but nonetheless welcome, were transferred to the Royal Navy.

P511 and P512, although operational, were de-rated for training. P511 operated from north east Scotland; P512 from Bermuda, on loan to the Royal Canadian Navy.

Loss

P514 was mistaken for U-boat and rammed by the Fleet minesweeper HMCS Georgian in the western Atlantic on 26 June 1942.

P552 on trials in the Clyde.

	launched	builder
P552 (ex *S1*)	1918	Fore River
P553 (ex *S21*), *P544* (ex *S22*)	1920	Bethlehem Shipbuilders
P555 (ex *S24*), *P556* (ex *S29*), *P551* (ex *S25*)	1922	Bethlehem Shipbuilders

Specification

Displacement	surfaced:	854 tons
	submerged:	1,062 tons
Dimensions:		211 wl × $20\frac{3}{4}$ × 16 ft
Complement:		42
Propulsion	surfaced:	Two diesel engines 1,200 bhp
	submerged:	Two electric motors 1,500 bhp
		Fuel capacity 400 tons
Speed	surfaced:	14 knots
	submerged:	11 knots
Range	surfaced:	8,000 nm at 10 knots
Armament	Gun:	Single 4 in
	Torpedo:	Four 21 in bow tubes

Class note: Supplied to the Royal Navy under the same terms as ex USN R Class.

Loss

P551 was mistaken for a U-boat off northern Norway and attacked by the destroyer *St Albans* and the minesweeper *Seagull* on 2 May 1942.

P614 off Rothesay.

	launched	builder
P611, P612, P614, P615	1940	Vickers Armstrong, Barrow-in-Furness

Specification

Displacement	surfaced:	683 tons
	submerged:	856 tons
Dimensions:		193 bp × 22¼ × 10½ ft
Complement:		41
Propulsion	surfaced:	Two diesel engines 1,550 bhp
	submerged:	Two electric motors 1,300 bhp
		Fuel capacity 40 tons
Speed	surfaced:	13¾ knots
	submerged:	10 knots
Range	surfaced:	6,500 nm
Armament	Gun:	Single 3 in
	Torpedo:	Five 21 in tubes, four internal bow, one external stern

Class note: These four boats were under construction for the Turkish Navy at the outbreak of World War II.

P611 and *P612* were required urgently by Turkey. It was arranged that they would be fully commissioned in the Royal Navy and 'work their passage' to Turkey. They were armed, but were not to seek the enemy, as their first priority was to reach their destination safely and speedily. They were also to carry important stores and personnel to Malta en route (though this was abandoned). Their departure from the Clyde was delayed for rectification of a design fault which made them unstable at submerged speeds over six knots, but they sailed on 26 March 1942. *P611* left Gibraltar on 7 April and thereafter travelled submerged by day with a planned passage of 100 miles a day. She reached Alexandria on 25 April (having reported a possible submarine on patrol off Algiers) and the Turkish naval base at Iskanderun on 9 May. *P612* had been delayed by a steering fault at Gibraltar and followed a week later. Their crews returned to the UK.

Before delivery to Turkey *P612* was used as a training boat at Portsmouth. *P614* and *P615* were also commissioned in the RN and were used for training in South Africa.

Under the Turkish flag they were *P611—Oruc Reis, P612—Murat Reis, P614—Burak Reis; P615* would have been named *Uluc Ali Reis.*

Loss

P615 was torpedoed by *U-123* off the west African coast on 15 April 1943.

	launched	builder
N46 (ex *U-570*)	1941	Blohm and Voss

Specification

Displacement	surfaced:	769 tons
	submerged:	871 tons
Dimensions:		213 bp × 20¼ × 15¾ ft
Complement:		44
Propulsion	surfaced:	Two diesel engines 2,800 bhp
	submerged:	Two electric motors 750 bhp
		Two shafts
Speed	surfaced:	17 knots
	submerged:	7½ knots
Armament	Gun:	Single 3.5 in; single 37 mm (AA); Two 20 mm (AA) in twin mounting
	Torpedo:	Five 21 in tubes, four bow, one stern

Graph (ex U-570) during evaluation in Scottish waters.

Class note: This was a standard Type VIIC U-boat, captured on 28 August 1941 after an attack by Coastal Command aircraft. Having been badly damaged in the first attack and being unable to dive because of flooding, she surrendered on the second attack. While aircraft maintained watch, the Royal Navy put on a boarding party and her crew were taken prisoner. This 'gift from the gods' as the Admiralty must have regarded her, was steamed with the aid of tugs to the UK to be thoroughly evaluated. She was then repaired and, as the RN was short of submarines, commissioned as HM S/M *Graph*, the name of the operation which had been her downfall. It was a similar fate to that suffered by *Seal*—see page 68.

Loss
On 20 March 1944 she was wrecked on the west coast of the Isle of Islay.

Another view of Graph.

Perla when she was commissioned in the Italian Navy.

	launched	builder
P711 (ex *Galileo Galilei*)	1934	Tosi

Specification

Displacement	surfaced:	880 tons
	submerged:	1,231 tons
Dimensions:		$231\frac{1}{4} \times 22\frac{1}{2} \times 13$ ft
Complement:		49
Propulsion	surfaced:	Two diesel engines 3,000 bhp
	submerged:	Two electric motors 1,300 bhp
Speed	surfaced:	17 knots
	submerged:	$8\frac{1}{2}$ knots
Armament	Gun:	Single 3.9 in, two 13 mm AA on single mountings
	Torpedo:	Eight 21 in tubes, four bow, four stern

	launched	builder
P712 (ex *Perla*)	1936	Adriatico

Specification

Displacement	surfaced:	620 tons
	submerged:	853 tons
Dimensions:		$197 \times 21 \times 13$ ft
Complement:		41
Propulsion	surfaced:	Two diesel engines 1,350 bhp
	submerged:	Two electric motors 800 bhp
Speed	surfaced:	14 knots
	submerged:	8 knots
Armament	Gun:	as *P711*
	Torpedo:	Six 21 in bow tubes

Bronzo when in commission with the Italian Navy.

	launched	builder
P714 (ex *Bronzo*)	1941	Tosi

Specification

Displacement	surfaced:	629 tons
	submerged:	864 tons
Dimensions:		$197\frac{1}{4} \times 21\frac{1}{4} \times 15\frac{1}{2}$ ft
Complement		48
Propulsion:		as *P712*
Speed	surfaced:	$14\frac{1}{2}$ knots
	submerged:	7 knots
Armament	Gun:	Single 3.9 in, four 13 mm AA on two twin mountings
	Torpedo:	Six 21 in tubes, four bow, two stern

Class note: *P711* had been attacked and disabled by the anti-submarine trawler *Moonstone* on 19 June 1940. She was taken into Aden and later to Alexandria for evaluation and was commissioned into the Royal Navy for use in training in the Mediterranean and the East Indies.

P712 was captured at Augusta, Sicily, on 9 July 1942. After evaluation she was commissioned as an operational boat and served in the Mediterranean until the end of World War II.

P714 was captured at Augusta, Sicily, on 12 July 1943. After evaluation she was commissioned as an operational boat in the Mediterranean. In 1944 she was transferred to the French Navy.

An X craft on trials.

X Prototype Class

	built	builder
X3, X4	1942	Varley Marine

Specification

Displacement	surfaced:	27 tons
	submerged:	30 tons
Dimensions:		$50 \times 5\frac{1}{2} \times 5\frac{1}{2}$ ft
Complement:		3
Propulsion	surfaced:	Diesel engine 42 bhp
	submerged:	Electric motor 25 bhp
Speed	surfaced:	$6\frac{1}{2}$ knots
	submerged:	$4\frac{1}{2}$ knots
Range	surfaced:	1,100 nm
	submerged:	85 nm
Armament:		'Side cargoes', port and starboard; limpet mines

X Operational Class

	built	builder
X5, X6	1942	Vickers Armstrong, Barrow-in-Furness
X7–X9	1943	Vickers Armstrong, Barrow-in-Furness

Specification

Displacement:		as Prototype Class
Dimensions:		$51\frac{1}{4} \times 5\frac{3}{4} \times 5\frac{3}{4}$ ft
Complement:		4
Propulsion:	surfaced:	Diesel engine 42 bhp
	submerged:	Electric motor 30 bhp
Speed	surfaced:	$6\frac{1}{2}$ knots
	submerged:	$5\frac{1}{2}$ knots
Range	surfaced:	1,300 nm
	submerged:	80 nm
Armament:		as Prototype Class

XE Operational Class (Pacific)

	built	builder
XE1–XE12	1944–5	Consortium of Broadbent, Markham (Chesterfield) and Marshall (Gainsborough)
XE20–XE25	1944	Vickers Armstrong, Barrow-in-Furness

Specification

Displacement	surfaced:	30 tons
	submerged:	34 tons
Dimensions:		$53 \times 5\frac{3}{4} \times 5\frac{3}{4}$ ft
Propulsion:		as X5–X9
Speed	surfaced:	$6\frac{1}{2}$ knots
	submerged:	6 knots
Range	surfaced:	1,800 nm
	submerged:	130 nm
Armament:		as X5–X9

XT Training Class

	built	builder
XT1–XT6	1944	Vickers Armstrong, Barrow-in-Furness

Specification as XE Class

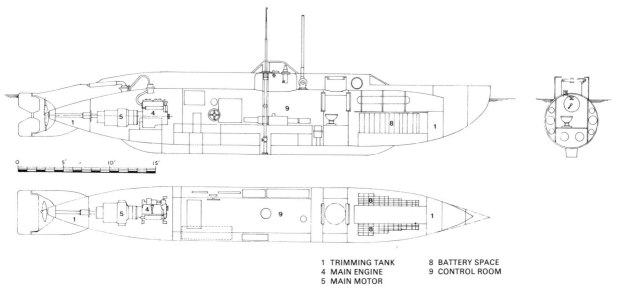

1	TRIMMING TANK	8	BATTERY SPACE
4	MAIN ENGINE	9	CONTROL ROOM
5	MAIN MOTOR		

An XT craft after completion by Vickers.

	built	builder
X Class (post war)		
X51–X54 (Minnow,		
Stickleback, Shrimp and		
Sprat)	1954	Vickers Armstrong,
		Barrow-in-Furness

Specification

Displacement	surfaced:	36 tons
	submerged:	41 tons
Dimensions:		$53\frac{3}{4} \times 6\frac{1}{4} \times 7\frac{1}{2}$ ft
Complement:		5
Propulsion	surfaced:	6 cyl diesel engine
	submerged:	Electric motors
		One shaft
Speed	surfaced:	7 knots
	submerged:	6 knots
Armament:		As XE Class
Cancellation:		*X10* was cancelled when partially built

Minnow with her free-flooding side cargoes fitted.

Class notes: The idea of a midget submarine may have been evolved from the successes by Italian naval personnel in disabling Royal Naval ships in Alexandria harbour in the earlier part of World War II. The first two X craft were built as prototypes by a company which had never built submarines before. They were much too small to carry torpedoes and their size was governed by the object of entering heavily guarded and secluded bases and harbours of the enemy. It will be noted from the dimensions that no man could stand upright in one of these craft. When being 'driven' on the surface, the commanding officer stood on the casing with a harness to secure him; and steering and other controls were through a mechanical rod device which, on submergence, folded flat on top of the hull. The periscope was 2 in in diameter and only had a single eyepiece.

The armament of these boats lay in the side cargoes, metal cased two-three ton charges of HE which was secured to the submarine by a threaded bolt. This was released from inside the hull by turning a hand wheel. The craft would manoeuvre close to its target, release its side cargo, which included a timing device, and move away before the charge exploded against the harbour bed and the ship's bottom.

X craft were also fitted with a wet-and-dry compartment which enabled one of the crew, suitably clad with underwater breathing gear and armed with limpet mines, to emerge from the boat and swim to the enemy vessel. The limpet mines attached themselves by magnets, but if the enemy ship's bottom was rather foul, the diver had the dangerous job of scraping away the barnacles to give a surface which the mines would hold.

The method of transport for X craft to the scene of attack was varied. They could be towed to within a few miles by a conventional submarine; they could be suspended underneath a vessel for short ranges; or they could be launched from the deck of a larger submarine or surface vessel. The craft were not particularly stable when under tow and the systems had to be monitored. A 'passage crew' controlled the boat, when under tow.

XE24 is preserved at the Royal Naval Submarine Museum, HMS *Dolphin*.

3	MAIN ENGINE ROOM	9	CONTROL ROOM
4	MAIN ENGINE	10	CREW ACCOMMODATION
5	MAIN MOTOR	20	MAIN BALLAST TANK

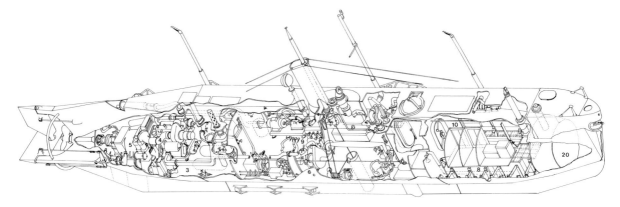

Losses

The following is understood to be accurate from the information available:

X5, X6 and *X7* were lost on 22 September 1943 during an attack on the German battleship *Tirpitz* in Altenfjord, Norway.

X8 was scuttled whilst approaching the Norwegian coast on 17 September 1943.

X10 was scuttled whilst approaching the Norwegian Coast on 3 October 1943.

X9 foundered whilst under tow in the North Sea on 15 October 1943.

*X22** collided with the HM S/M *Syrtis* in the Pentland Firth on 7 February 1944.

XE11 was in collision with a boom defence vessel on 6 March 1945.

*XE 22** was in collision in the Pentland Firth with an unknown
• vessel and lost on 7 February 1944.

*It is uncertain if both *X22* and *XE 22* were lost; Vickers' Yard List shows *XE22* as having been commissioned 31 October 1943 and lost as above. No further details are given.

Stickleback in use as a training boat at Gosport.

X51, later Minnow, when she was operational.

Specification

Displacement:		4,540 lbs (5,740 lbs with charge)
Dimensions:		$17\frac{1}{4}$ ($20\frac{1}{2}$ with charge) $\times 3\frac{1}{2} \times 4\frac{1}{2}$ ft
Complement:		1
Propulsion	surfaced:	Internal combustion engine
	submerged:	Electric motor
Speed	surfaced:	3 knots
Armament:		Single charge of 1,200 lbs (of which 600 lbs was HE)

Welfreighter (Marks I–III)
Specification Similar to Welman craft, but designed to have two crew and carry 200 lbs cargo in place of armament.

Class note: The Welman one-man submarine was unique to the Royal Navy. It was invented by Col. Dolphin (co-incidentally the same name as the Royal Navy submarine base at Gosport) and was built at a hotel in Welwyn Garden City, from which it derives its name. The first two craft were built at 'Station IX' between June and August 1942.

The intention was that they would be a weapon against shipping in harbour or, in the Welfreighter mode, used for survey and beach reconnaissance, or to carry stores and weapons to resistance movements in occupied territories.

The craft were strongly built, as is evidenced by a trial in which one was lowered to a depth of 100 ft before imploding. They were, however, slow and had a short range. The HE charge was fixed to the bow and released by a mechanical gear after magnetically attaching to the target.

The Welfreighter building programme commenced in November 1942; trials began at Staines in July 1943 and at Fishguard in March 1944. Six craft were ordered with Shelvoke and Drewry in June 1944. The number was increased to 40, but it is not known if all were completed. Twelve craft were shipped

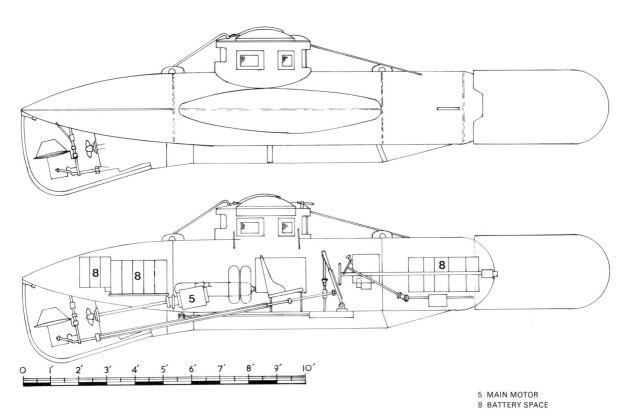

0 1' 2' 3' 4' 5' 6' 7' 8' 9' 10'

5 MAIN MOTOR
8 BATTERY SPACE

to Australia in mid-1945 (one, at least, being 'driven' round the Garden Island Navy Yard).

Had the craft been used operationally in Europe they would have been crewed by SOE (Special Operations Executive) personnel.

Only one naval action is recorded in which Welman craft took part. This was an attack by four craft (Nos 45–48) on Bergen harbour on 20–22 November 1943. They were crewed by Lt. J. P. L. Holmes, RN, Lt. V. M. Harris, RNVR, Lt. C. A. Johnson and 2nd Lt. H. Petersen of the Royal Norwegian Army. They were carried to the target area by MTBs, but mis-timed their arrival and were forced to spend over a day in hiding near an island outside the harbour where they were seen by local fishermen. Whether or not for that reason, they found the defences extremely alert when the operation was begun. The first craft was captured and the other three found it impossible to press home their attack despite repeated attempts. The craft were scuttled and the crews made their way ashore where they were aided by the local population. They were finally rescued by MTBs from Shetland on 5 February 1944.

A Welman Mk III about to be launched, complete with warhead, into a Scottish harbour.

	completed	*builder*
N35 U-2326 (Type XXIII)	1945	Deutsche Werft, Hamburg

Four U-boats of the same type as U-2326 moored at Lishahally, Ulster, where they came after surrendering. They were of a remarkably modern streamlined design.

Specification

Displacement	surfaced:	232 tons
	submerged:	256 tons
Dimensions:		$112 \times 9\frac{1}{2} \times 13$ ft
Complement:		14
Propulsion	surfaced:	Diesel engine 580 bhp
	submerged:	Electric motor 600 bhp
		Electric 'creeping' motor 35 shp
Speed	surfaced:	$9\frac{1}{2}$ knots
	submerged:	$12\frac{1}{2}$ knots; 'creeping' speed 2 knots
Range	surfaced:	1,400 nm at $9\frac{1}{2}$ knots
	submerged:	175 nm at 4 knots
Armament	Torpedo:	Two 21 in bow tubes

A submarine of the same type as U-3017. She has a sonar dome half way along the fore casing and a streamlined conning tower.

		completed	builder
N41 U-3017 (Type XXI)		1945	Deschimag, Bremen

Specification

Displacement	surfaced:	1,612 tons
	submerged:	1,819 tons
Dimensions:		251 × 21¾ × 20 ft
Complement:		57
Propulsion	surfaced:	Two diesel engines 4,000 bhp
	submerged:	Two electric motors 5,000 bhp
		Two electric 'creeping' motors 226 shp
Speed	surfaced:	15½ knots
	submerged:	16 knots; 'creeping speed' 6 knots
Range	surfaced:	11,150 nm at 12 knots
	submerged:	285 nm at 6 knots
Armament	Gun:	Four 30 mm on two twin mountings (AA)
	Torpedo:	Six 21 in bow tubes 23 reloads or
	Mines:	12 with 12 torpedo reloads

Class note: Under pennant No *N35, U-2326* was evaluated and handed over to the French Navy in 1946. On 6 December 1946 she was accidentally lost off Toulon.

Under Pennant No *N41, U-3017* was in commission for evaluation from August to September 1945 and was scrapped in 1949.

Aeneas on builder's trials in the Mersey.

	launched	builder
Achates	1945	HM Dockyard, Devonport
Acheron	1945	HM Dockyard, Chatham
Aeneas, Affray	1945	Cammell Laird
Alaric	1946	Cammell Laird
Alcide, Alderney, Alliance, Ambush	1945	Vickers Armstrong, Barrow-in-Furness
Amphion (later Anchorite)	1946	Vickers Armstrong, Barrow-in-Furness
Anchorite (later Amphion)	1944	Vickers Armstrong, Barrow-in-Furness
Andrew	1946	Vickers Armstrong, Barrow-in-Furness
Artemis	1946	Scotts
Artful	1947	Scotts
Astute, Auriga, Aurochs	1945	Vickers Armstrong, Barrow-in-Furness

Cancellations: The following 28 boats were cancelled. *Abelard, Acasta* (HM Dockyard, Portsmouth); *Ace* (HM Dockyard, Devonport); *Adept* (HM Dockyard, Chatham); *Andromache, Answer, Antaeus, Antagonist, Anzac, Aphrodite, Approach, Arcadian, Ardent, Argosy* (Vickers Armstrong, Barrow-in-Furness); *Admirable,*

Adversary, Asperity, Austere, Awake, Aztec (Vickers Armstrong, Newcastle upon Tyne); *Azgard, Assurance, Astarte* (Scotts); *Agate, Aggressor, Agile, Aladdin, Alcestis* (Cammell Laird)

Specification

Displacement	surfaced:	1,385 tons
	submerged:	1,620 tons
Dimensions:		$281\frac{1}{2} \times 22\frac{1}{4} \times 17$ ft
Complement:		60
Propulsion	surfaced:	Two diesels, 430 hp
	submerged:	Two electric motors, 1,250 hp
Speed	surfaced:	18 knots
	submerged:	8 knots
Fuel capacity:		300 tons
Armament	Gun:	One 4 in, one 20 mm
	Torpedo:	Ten 21 in tubes; four internal and two external in the bow; two internal and two external in the stern
	Mines:	20 or 26
Range:		10,500 nm at 11 knots

A Class submarines in various stages of completion at Vickers yard.

A CLASS (1945) (continued)

Astute after her first refit showing all the wartime innovations.

Class notes: The first boat of this class, *Amphion,* was a little unstable therefore a bow buoyancy tank was fitted.

This Class was intended for long-range patrol work, particularly in the war against the Japanese, but the majority of the boats were completed after the cessation of hostilities.

Loss
Affray failed to surface in the English Channel on 17 April 1951.

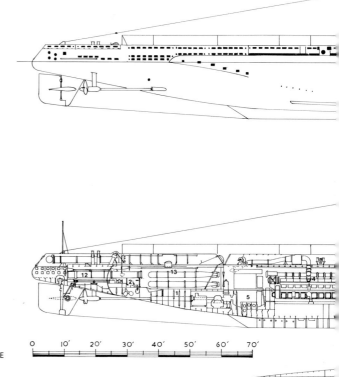

1 TRIMMING TANK	15 FORWARD TORPEDO TUBES
2 STEERING GEAR COMPARTMENT	16 FORWARD TORPEDO STOWAGE
3 MAIN ENGINE ROOM	17 FUEL TANKS
4 MAIN ENGINE	19 RADIO ROOM
5 MAIN MOTOR	20 MAIN BALLAST TANK
8 BATTERY SPACE	23 'Q' TANK
9 CONTROL ROOM	25 SEARCH PERISCOPE
10 CREW ACCOMMODATION	26 ATTACK PERISCOPE
11 WARD ROOM	28 RADAR MAST
12 AFTER TORPEDO TUBES	29 4 in GUN
13 AFTER TORPEDO STOWAGE	

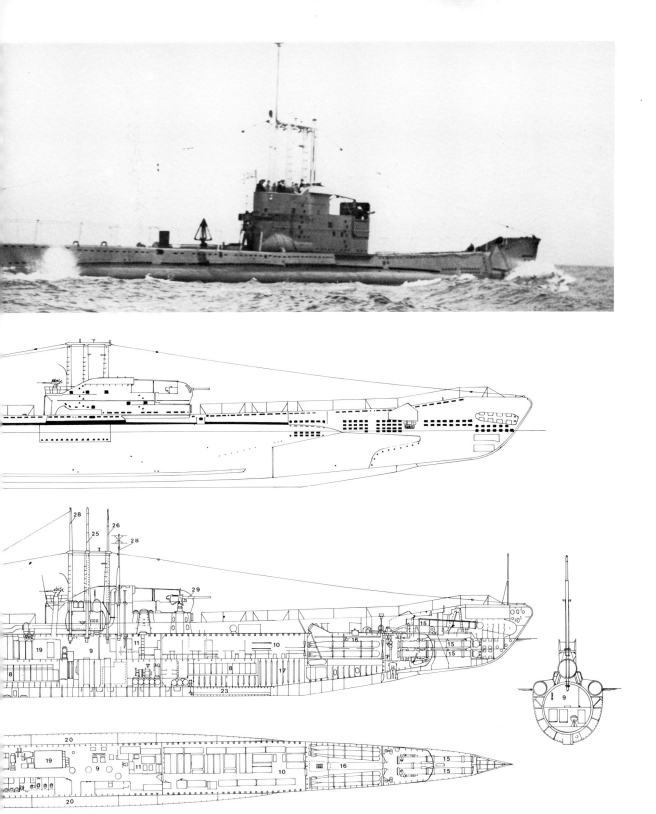

Grampus on builder's trials (as she is wearing the Red Ensign). The bollards fore and aft are retractable.

	commenced	completed	builder
Cachalot	1955	1959	Scotts
Finwhale	1956	1960	Cammell Laird
Grampus	1955	1958	Cammell Laird
Narwhal	1956	1959	Vickers Armstrong, Barrow-in-Furness
Porpoise	1954	1958	Vickers Armstrong, Barrow-in-Furness
Rorqual	1955	1958	Vickers Armstrong, Barrow-in-Furness
Sealion	1958	1961	Cammell Laird
Walrus	1958	1961	Scotts

Specification

Displacement	surfaced:	2,030 tons
	submerged:	2,405 tons
Dimensions:		241 bp $\times$ 26$\frac{1}{2}$ $\times$ 18 ft
Complement:		71
Propulsion	surfaced:	Two diesel engines, 3,680 bhp
	submerged:	Two electric motors, 6,000 shp
Speed	surfaced:	12 knots
	submerged:	17 knots
Range:		9,000 nm at 12 knots
Armament	Torpedo:	Eight 21 in tubes, six bow, two stern* 30 reloads

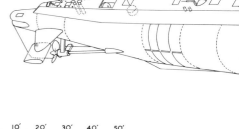

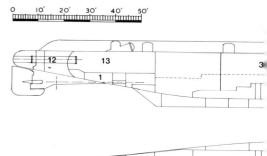

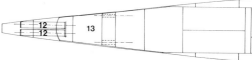

* In some boats the stern tubes were modified to five 12$\frac{3}{4}$ in torpedoes.

Class note: This was the first major Class to be built for the Royal Navy after World War II. The boats were substantially remodelled in structure and outline from the A and T Classes.

Armament note: From this Class, with the exception of a small number of boats that carried a gun during the period of the Indonesian confrontation, deck guns were no longer mounted. A deck gun in kit form with portable mountings may be stowed in the hull.

This class, and some of the later 'A' Class, incorporated the 'Snort' underwater breathing system. The *Porpoise* and *Oberon* Classes are probably the most efficient conventional powered submarines in the world today. They are noted for their near-silent running. A maximum diving depth of 1,000 ft is understood to be possible.

1	TRIMMING TANK	15	FORWARD TORPEDO TUBES
3	MAIN ENGINE ROOM	16	FORWARD TORPEDO STOWAGE
8	BATTERY SPACE	24	'SNORT' MAST
9	CONTROL ROOM	25	SEARCH PERISCOPE
10	CREW ACCOMMODATION	26	ATTACK PERISCOPE
12	AFTER TORPEDO TUBES	27	W/T MAST
13	AFTER TORPEDO STOWAGE	28	RADAR MAST

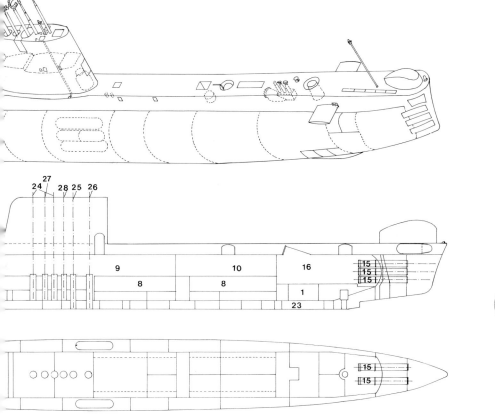

PORPOISE CLASS (continued)

Finwhale on builder's trials in the Clyde.

Sealion prepares to dive into the sunset.

Meteorite at speed, clearly showing the effect of her HTP power system.

		launched	builder
Meteorite (ex *U-1407*)		*c.* 1943	Blohm and Voss, Hamburg

Specification

Displacement	surfaced:	312 tons
	submerged:	357 tons
Dimensions:		$136 \times 11\frac{1}{4} \times 14$ ft
Complement:		19
Propulsion	surfaced:	Diesel engine 210 bhp
		Walther HTP turbine 2,500 shp
	submerged:	Electric motor 77 bhp
Speed	surfaced:	Diesel power $8\frac{1}{2}$ knots; turbine 20 knots
	submerged:	5 knots (turbine 20 knots)
Range:	surfaced:	Diesel power 3,000 nm at 8 knots, turbine 115 nm at 20 knots
	submerged:	40 nm at $4\frac{1}{2}$ knots
Armament	Torpedo:	Two 21 in bow tubes, four reloads

Note: This boat was found scuttled at Cuxhaven by RN Occupation forces. She was raised in May 1945 for evaluation of the Walther HTP turbine (see below). Vickers were given the task of carrying out trials, the results of which were sufficiently encouraging for the Admiralty to order building of the EX Class.

Meteorite was broken up in 1950.

The Walther Turbine High Test Peroxide system was an advanced experimental means of submarine propulsion developed by the German Navy and first tested in the 80-ton *V80* in 1940. Trials were successful and the HTP system was planned for *V-300*, later *U-791*. This was not carried out, but the system was added to a number of Type VII boats then being built.

The principle of the HTP system was a closed-circuit turbine powered by gas independent of the external atmosphere. The gas was generated from the decomposition in water of concentrated hydrogen peroxide (Penhydral or Ingolin) which produced a hot gas at very high pressure. Fuel consumption was high and the compound unstable.

U-1407 after being raised at Cuxhaven.

Explorer leaving Vickers yard for trials.

	launched	completed	builder
Explorer	1954	1956	Vickers Armstrong, Barrow-in-Furness
Excalibur	1955	1958	Vickers Armstrong, Barrow-in-Furnace

Specification

Displacement	surfaced:	780 tons
	submerged:	1,000 tons
Dimensions:		$225\frac{1}{2} \times 15\frac{1}{2} \times 11$
Complement:		*Explorer* 49, *Excalibur* 41
Propulsion:		These submarines were unique in having three differing power systems: diesel engines, electric motors, and steam turbines driven by heat from HTP fuel reaction
Speed	surfaced:	15 knots
	submerged:	30 knots
Armament:		Nil

Class note: These boats were built as experimental submarines for full-scale investigation and testing of hydrogen peroxide fuel. This provided superior power to conventional machinery and was practically noiseless. The experiments continued until 1968 (*Excalibur* was scrapped in 1970) but the fuel compound proved to be so unstable that, as in the early A and B Classes with their petrol engines, the fuel was more dangerous to the boat than the benefits accrued. The idea of hydrogen peroxide power came from investigations and tests into its use by the German Navy (see p. 101). The system was evaluated by the Admiralty in great depth as is evidenced by the building of these two submarines.

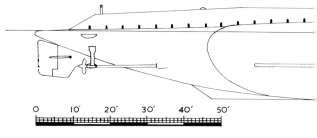

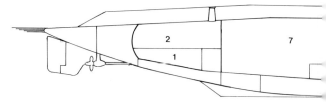

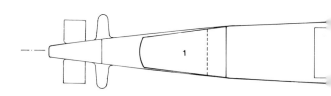

1 TRIMMING TANK
2 STEERING GEAR COMPARTMENT
5 MAIN MOTOR
6 FEED WATER
7 TURBINE ROOM
8 BATTERY SPACE
9 CONTROL ROOM
10 CREW ACCOMMODATION
20 MAIN BALLAST TANK
21 DIESEL ROOM
23 'Q' TANK

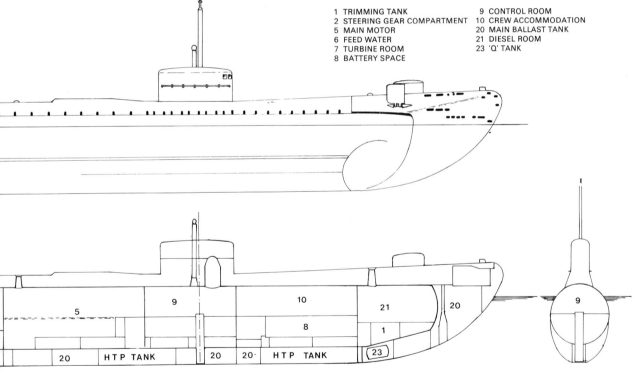

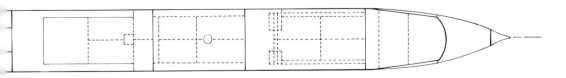

Onslaught in the Gare Loch showing a turn of speed.

	commenced	completed	builder
Oberon	1957	1961	HM Dockyard, Chatham
Ocelot	1960	1964	HM Dockyard, Chatham
Odin	1959	1962	Cammell Laird
Olympus	1960	1962	Vickers Armstrong, Barrow-in-Furness
Onslaught	1959	1962	HM Dockyard, Chatham
Onyx (II)	1964	1967	Cammell Laird
Opossum	1961	1964	Cammell Laird
Opportune	1961	1964	Scotts
Oracle	1960	1963	Cammell Laird
Orpheus	1959	1960	Vickers Armstrong, Barrow-in-Furness
Osiris	1962	1964	Vickers Armstrong, Barrow-in-Furness
Otter	1960	1962	Scotts
Otus	1961	1963	Scotts

Class note: *Onyx 1* was sold to Canada after commissioning and re-named *Ojibwa*. This Class followed a similar design to the Porpoise Class, but with differences in the frames of the pressure hull. Parts of the conning tower were constructed of plastic or glass fibre—it has been reported that some elderly submariners 'found it strange to see the sun shining through the conning tower for a change'.† The conning tower of *Orpheus* is constructed of aluminium.

Like the Porpoise Class, this Class is said to be able to submerge to 1,000 ft.

*Warships of the Royal Navy, 1979.

Specification

Displacement	surfaced:	2,030 tons
	submerged:	2,410 tons
Dimensions:		$295\frac{1}{4} \times 26\frac{1}{2} \times 18$ ft
Complement:		68
Propulsion	surfaced:	Two diesel engines 3,680 bhp
	submerged:	Two electric motors 6,000 shp
Speed	surfaced:	12 knots
	submerged:	17 knots
Range:		9,000 nm at 12 knots
Armament	Torpedo:	Eight 21 in: six bow and two stern tubes* 24 reloads

*In some boats the stern tubes were modified to five $12\frac{3}{4}$ in torpedoes.
†*Warships of the Royal Navy*, 1979.

Odin moving smoothly in a calm sea.

	launched	completed	builder
Dreadnought	1960	1963	Vickers Armstrong, Barrow-in-Furness

Specification

Displacement	surfaced:	3,500 tons
	submerged:	4,000 tons
Dimensions:		$256\frac{3}{4}$ bp $\times 32\frac{1}{4} \times 26$ ft
Complement:		88
Propulsion	surfaced:	Geared steam turbines 15,000 shp
	submerged:	powered from pressurised water-cooled nuclear reactor
Speed	submerged:	Better than 28 knots
Range:		100,000 nm (approx)
Armament	Torpedo:	Six 21 in bow tubes

Class note: This submarine in much of her design was similar to the *Skipjack* Class of the US Navy. The US government authorising the supply of reactor, propulsion plant and the requisite design knowhow, the hull being very largely the work of Admiralty and Vickers designers and constructors. This is a 'one-boat' Class and is the first true nuclear submarine to be built for the Royal Navy. She was taken out of commission in 1982. She was the first British submarine to surface under the ice at the North Pole (in 1971).

The name *Dreadnought* carries twelve Battle Honours from Armada (1588) to Trafalgar (1805).

Nuclear power gives a number of advantages, including high speed and high power, fresh water as required, no danger under depth-charge attack from external fuel tanks, and no limit to time submerged by reason of lack of fresh air.

Armament note: In 1980 *Dreadnought* was fitted with the Harpoon missile system (see Appendix G, p. 122).

Left
Dreadnought nearly awash. An early photograph, as she is wearing the Red Ensign and pennant numbers are no longer painted on the conning tower.

Right
The slim silhouette of Dreadnought's conning tower.

Below
Dreadnought with her hydroplanes angled upward, their position when not in use.

Warspite on trials. Very similar to Dreadnought in appearance.

	launched	completed	builder
Valiant	1962	1966	Vickers Shipbuilders, Barrow-in-Furness
Warspite	1963	1967	Vickers Shipbuilders, Barrow-in-Furness

Specification

Displacement	surfaced:	3,500 tons
	submerged:	4,500 tons
Dimensions:		$285 \times 33\frac{1}{4} \times 27$ ft
Complement:		103
Propulsion:		Geared steam turbine to one shaft powered by single water-cooled nuclear reactor 15,000 shp
Speed	submerged:	Better than 28 knots
Range:		Approx 80,000 nm
Armament	Torpedo:	Six 21 in bow tubes; 26 re-loads

Class note: A recurring problem in these boats (and in similar Classes in the US Navy) was hairline cracks in the welding which were to very fine tolerances. New welding techniques were developed to overcome the difficulty but frequent dry-docking was necessary.

Valiant completed the record submerged voyage of 12,000 nm from Singapore to UK in April 1967. The voyage took 28 days.

Armament note: In 1980 the Class was fitted with the Harpoon missile sytem.

Valiant, sister to Warspite, digging in her bows.

	launched	completed	builder
Resolution	1964	1967	Vickers Shipbuilding, Barrow-in-Furness
Repulse	1965	1968	Vickers Shipbuilding, Barrow-in-Furness
Renown	1964	1968	Cammell Laird
Revenge	1965	1969	Cammell Laird

One further boat was planned but construction not commenced

Repulse in Plymouth Sound. The design of the hydroplanes should be compared with those in other nuclear powered submarines.

Propulsion:		Geared steam turbine powered by single pressurised water-cooled nuclear reactor
Speed	submerged:	Better than 25 knots
Range:		Approx 100,000 nm
Armament	Torpedo:	Six 21 in bow tubes
	Missiles:	Sixteen Polaris A3 (see Armament note)

Specification

Displacement	surfaced:	7,500 tons
	submerged:	8,400 tons
Dimensions:		360 bp × 33 × 30 ft
Complement:		143 (see Class note)

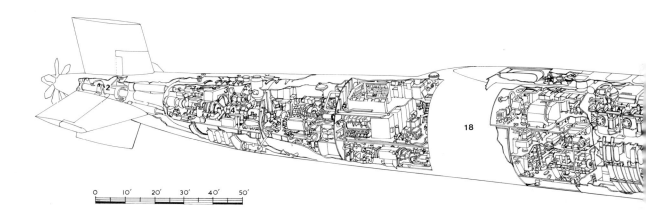

0   10'   20'   30'   40'   50'

Class note: Following the precedent set by the US Navy, these Polaris armed submarines are used as the UK nuclear deterrent because of the vulnerability of the manned bomber to anti-aircraft attack and because the land forces do not possess a strategic nuclear weapon.

These boats normally carry out a two-month patrol before returning for a short service. As this imposes a considerable strain on one crew, two are attached to each boat (known as the Port and Starboard crews) which alternate after each patrol. The seagoing limitations of earlier submarines are thus transferred from the boats to the crews.

A new Class has been proposed to replace the Resolution Class. It is planned that there will be four boats to be built by Vickers Shipbuilding and Engineering Ltd of which the first is to be laid down in 1986 for commissioning in 1993. Displacement is planned to be 14,680 tons; propulsion to be from a pressurised water reactor system. The boats would have a refit interval of seven years. They would be armed with 16 Trident D5 missiles, with a range of 6,000 nm and each missile would carry 14 independently targeted warheads.

Armament note: The Polaris missiles each carry three Chevaline (Chevaline means 'mountain goat') independently targeted warheads.

2 STEERING GEAR COMPARTMENT
3 MAIN ENGINE ROOM
9 CONTROL ROOM
10 CREW ACCOMMODATION
11 WARD ROOM

24 'SNORT' MAST
25 SEARCH PERISCOPE
26 ATTACK PERISCOPE
28 RADAR MAST
31 SONAR ROOM

Resolution from the stern, giving a good idea of her bulk.

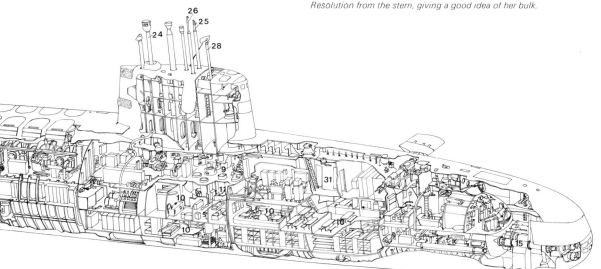

Churchill on trials.

	launched	completed	builder
Churchill	1967	1970	Vickers Shipbuilding, Barrow-in-Furness
Conqueror	1967	1971	Cammell Laird
Courageous	1968	1971	Vickers Shipbuilding, Barrow-in-Furness

Specification

Displacement	surfaced:	3,500 tons
	submerged:	4,500 tons
Dimensions:		$285 \times 33\frac{1}{4} \times 27$ ft
Complement:		103
Propulsion:		Geared steam turbine to one shaft powered by single pressurised water-cooled nuclear reactor
Speed	submerged:	Better than 28 knots
Range:		Approx 80,000 nm
Armament	Torpedo:	Six 21 in bow tubes (26 reloads) (see armament note)

Class note: This was to have been part of the Valiant Class but, by Defence Council instruction, August 1979, it was decided to form a new Class.

Conqueror was one of the Royal Navy submarines involved in the Falklands conflict and sank the Argentine cruiser *General Belgrano* with two Tigerfish torpedoes on 2 May 1982.

Armament note: Rapid torpedo reloading equipment allows reloading in 15 seconds. In 1980 the Class was fitted with Harpoon missile system.

Conqueror, showing the speed and power with which she is being propelled and the wave formation created by her hull form.

Launch photograph of Courageous showing her whale-shaped hull.

Swiftsure cruising off the Scottish coast.

	launched	completed	builder
Sovereign	1970	1974	The whole Class built
Superb	1972	1976	by Vickers Shipbuilding,
Sceptre	1973	1978	Barrow-in-Furness
Spartan	1976	1979	
Splendid	1977	1981	
Swiftsure	1969	1973	

Specification

Displacement	surfaced:	4,000 tons
	submerged:	4,500 tons
Dimensions:		$272 \times 32\frac{1}{4} \times 27$ ft
Complement:		97
Propulsion:		Geared steam turbine powered by single pressurised water-cooled nuclear reactor 15,000 shp Diesel engine 4,000 hp (auxiliary)
Speed	submerged:	Better than 30 knots
Range:		Approx 75,000 nm
Armament	Torpedo:	Five 21 in bow tubes (20 reloads)

Class note: This Class is similar to the Valiant Class but has a shorter hull. The hydroplanes are further forward and the Class has deeper diving capability.

Armament note: Fast reloading capability enables torpedoes to be loaded in 15 seconds. In 1980 the Class was fitted with the Harpoon missile system.

Sceptre exercising with a Wessex helicopter.

	launched	builder
Trafalgar	1981	Vickers Shipbuilding, Barrow-in-Furness
Turbulent	—	Vickers Shipbuilding, Barrow-in-Furness
Planned:		_Tactician, Talent, Tireless, Torbay_

Specification

Displacement	surfaced:	4,800 tons
	submerged:	6,200 tons
Dimensions:		Length: 272 ft
Complement:		98
Propulsion:		Geared steam turbine to one shaft powered by single pressurised water-cooled nuclear reactor 18,000 shp
Speed	submerged:	Better than 25 knots
Diving depth:		Greater than 500 ft
Armament	Torpedo:	Five 21 in tubes (see Armament note)
	Missile:	Harpoon

Class note: This Class is to be fitted with noise-insulating tiles on the hull to reduce the amount of noise emitted, one of the principal means of submarine detection. The Class will thus be much quieter than the Swiftsure Class.

Reactor endurance is intended to be two-three years though in peacetime patrols will probably be limited to two months.

Armament note: The torpedo armament includes Tigerfish wire-guided homing torpedoes in addition to the unguided type.

	builder
	Vickers Shipbuilding, Barrow-in-Furness

Proposed specification

Displacement	surfaced:	2,160 tons
	submerged:	2,400 tons
Dimensions:		230 × 25 ft
Complement:		44–46
Propulsion:		Diesel electric: two diesel generators 4,000 hp powering single twin armature electric motor 4,000 kW
Speed	surfaced:	12 knots
	submerged:	20 knots
Range:		8,000 nm at 8 knots, snorting depth
Endurance:		Twenty-eight days at cruising speed
Diving depth:		Better than 600 feet
Armament	Torpedo:	Six 21 in tubes (12 reloads)
	Missile:	Harpoon Minelaying capability

Class note: This design is the first using diesel power since the Oberon Class of 1961–7 and _Onyx (II)_ completed in 1967. The first of this Class (provisionally named _Upholder_) is planned to be operational by 1986.

The launch of Trafalgar. The angular metal cover on the bows is a security measure to conceal the weapon exits.

APPENDIX A: Royal Navy submarines lost in peacetime

Holland *No 5*	*K5*
A1	*K15*
A2	*L9*
A3	*L23*
A4	*L24*
A7	*L55*
A8	*M1*
B2	*Poseidon*
C11	*Affray*
C14	*Sidon*
G11	*Sportsman*
H4	*Safari*
H29	*Thetis*
H42	*Truculent*
H43	*Truant*
H47	

Causes of loss:

Collision 12
Sea hazard 6
Accident 2
Gunfire 1
Other cause 9
Total 31

APPENDIX B: Royal Navy Submarines lost 1914–18

A1	*E5*	*E34*
A2	*E6*	*E36*
B10	*E7*	*E37*
C3	*E8*	*E47*
C26	*E9*	*E49*
C27	*E10*	*E50*
C29	*E13*	*G7*
C31	*E14*	*G8*
C32	*E15*	*G9*
C33	*E16*	*H3*
C34	*E17*	*H5*
C35	*E18*	*H6*
D2	*E19*	*H10*
D3	*E20*	*J6*
D5	*E22*	*K1*
D6	*E24*	*K4*
E1	*E26*	*K17*
E3	*E30*	*L10*

Causes of loss:

Surface action 3
Submarine 4
Mined 4
Destroyed to avoid capture 9
Blockship 1*
Collision 4
Wrecked 4
Accident 4
Unknown 21
Total 54

*Blown up at Zeebrugge Mole.

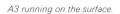

A3 running on the surface.

APPENDIX C: German U-Boats sunk by RN submarines 1914-1918

U-Boat	Date	Location	HM S/M
U-6	15.9.15	North Sea	E16
U-23	20.7.17	North Sea	C27 and HMS Princess Louise
U-40	23.6.15	off Girdle Ness	C24 and HM trawler
U-45	12.9.17	off Malin Head	D7
U-51	14.7.16	Heligoland Bight	H5
U-78	28.10.18	North Sea	G2
U–154	11.5.18	off Cape St Vincent	E35
UB-16	10.5.18	North Sea	E34
UB-52	23.5.18	in the Adriatic	H4
UB-72	12.5.18	English Channel	D2
UB-90	16.10.18	off the Norwegian coast	L12
UC-10	6.7.15	off Schouwen Light Vessel	E54
UC-43	10.3.17	off Muckle Flugga Light House	G13
UC-62	10.17	off Lowestoft	E45
UC-63	1.11.17	Straits of Dover	E52
UC-65	3.11.17	Straits of Dover	C15
UC-68	5.4.17	North Sea	C7
UC-79	19.10.17	North Sea	E45

APPENDIX D: Royal Navy submarines and X-craft lost 1939–1945

B1 (ex Sunfish)	Phoenix	Thames
Cachalot	Porpoise	Thistle
Grampus	Rainbow	Thorn
H31	Regent	Thunderbolt
H49	Regulus	Tigris
Jastrzab (ex P551)	Sahib	Traveller
Narwhal	Salmon	Triad
Odin	Saracen	Triton
Olympus	Sea Horse	Triumph
Orpheus	Shark	Trooper
Oswald	Sickle	Turbulent
Oxley	Simoom	Umpire
P32	Snapper	Unbeaten
P33	Spearfish	Undaunted
P36	Splendid	Undine
P38	Starfish	Union
P39	Sterlet	Unique
P48	Stonehenge	Unity
P222	Stratagem	Untamed*
P311	Swordfish	Upholder
P514	Syrtis	Uredd (ex P41)
P715 (ex Graph)	Talisman	Urge
Pandora	Tarpon	Usk
Parthian	Tempest	Usurper
Perseus	Tetrarch	Utmost
		Vandal
		X Craft: 5–10, 22

*Subsequently salvaged and renamed Vitality.

Causes of Loss RN Submarines and X-craft, 1939–45

	Mined	Aircraft	Submarine	Surface action	Rammed	Enemy action cause unknown	Collision	Accident	Unknown	Own forces	Wrecked	Totals
S/M	23	5	4	13	2	—	1	5	20	2	1	76
XC	—	—	—	—	—	6	1	—	—	—	—	7
												83

APPENDIX E: German U-Boats sunk by RN submarines in World War II

U-Boat	Date	Location	HM S/M
U-1	16.4.40	North Sea	*Porpoise*
U-36	4.12.39	North Sea	*Salmon*
U-51	20.8.40	Bay of Biscay	*Cachalot*
U-54	12.4.40	North Sea	*Salmon*
U-301	21.1.43	off Corsica	*Sahib*
U-303	21.5.43	off Toulon	*Sickle*
U-308	4.6.43	north of the Faeroes	*Truculent*
U-335	3.8.42	north of the Faeroes	*Saracen*
U-374	12.1.42	off Catania	*Unbeaten*
U-431	30.10.43	off Toulon	*Ultimatum*
U-486	12.4.45	northwest of Bergen	*Tapir*
U-644	7.4.43	northwest of Narvik	*Tuna*
U-771	11.11.44	off the Lofoten Islands	*Venturer*
U-859	10.10.44	Straits of Malacca	*Trenchant*
U-987	15.6.44	west of Narvik	*Satyr*
U-864	9.2.45	west of Bergen	*Venturer*

Italian U-Boats sunk by RN submarines in World War II

U-Boat	Date	Location	HM S/M
Acciaio	13.7.43	Straits of Messina	*Unruly*
Ammiraglio Enrico Millo	14.3.42	off Calabria	*Ultimatum*
Ammiraglio St Bon	5.1.42	off Sicily	*Upholder*
Diamante	20.6.40	off Tobruk	*Parthian*
Graneto	9.11.42	off northwest Sicily	*Saracen*
Guglielmotti	17.3.42	off Sicily	*Unbeaten*
Jantina	5.7.41	off north coast of Egypt	*Torbay*
Medusa	30.1.42	Adriatic	*Thorn*
Michele Bianchi	7.10.41	Adriatic	*Severn*
Pier Capponi	31.3.41	off Sicily	*Rorqual*
Pietro Micca	29.7.43	Straits of Taranto	*Trooper*
Porfido	6.12.42	South of Sardinia	*Tigris*
Remo	15.7.43	Gulf of Taranto	*United*
Salpoa	27.1.41	off north coast of Egypt	*Triumph*
Capitano Tarantina	15.12.40	Bay of Biscay	*Thunderbolt*
Tricheco	18.3.42	Adriatic	*Upholder*
U-IT23 (ex Reginaldo Giuliani)	14.2.44	Malacca Straits	*Tally Ho*
Velella	7.9.43	Gulf of Salerno	*Shakespeare*

A German U-Boat under attack in World War II.

Japanese U-Boats sunk by RN submarines in World War II

U-Boat	Date	Location	HM S/M
I-34	13.11.43	Straits of Malacca	Taurus
I-166	17.7.44	off Perang	Telemachus

APPENDIX F: U-Boats taken over by the Royal Navy for evaluation 1939–1949

U-Boat No.	Type	Postwar Career
U-712	VIIC	Scrapped
U-795	XVII	Scrapped
U-926	VIIC	Transferred to Norway 1947 as Kya
U-953	VIIC	Broken up 1949
U-1057	VIIC	Transferred to Russia 1946
U-1058	VIIC	Transferred to Russia 1946
U-1064	VIIC	Transferred to Russia as S81
U-1105	VIIC 41/42	Later HM S/M N16
U-1171	VIIC 41/42	Later HM S/M N19
U-1202	VIIC 41/42	Transferred to Norway 1947 as Kynn
U-1407	XVIIB	Later HM S/M Meteorite
U-2326	XXIII	Later HM S/M N35 transferred to France 1946
U-2353	XXIII	Later HM S/M N31 transferred to Russia later
U-2518	XXI	Transferred to France 1947
U-2529	XXI	Later HM S/M N27. Transferred to Russia 1946
U-3017	XXI	Later HM S/M N41. Scrapped 1949
U-3035	XXI	Later HM S/M N28. Transferred to Russia 1946
U-3041	XXI	Later HM S/M N29. Transferred to Russia 1946
U-3515	XXI	Later HM S/M N30. Transferred to Russia 1946
U-4706	XXVI	Transferred to Norway as Knerter in 1948

U-1105 had been covered entirely by the Germans with a special rubber coating which it was hoped would absorb the asdic (sonar) pings, thus reducing the chances of detection. The Royal Navy ran this boat for some months in late 1945. It was then handed over to the US Navy, and after further trials was scuttled. Whilst in RN service the boat was nicknamed 'The Black Panther'.

Another of the boats, number so far unidentified, had a sponge rubber coating around the head of the Snorkel mast. The sponge rubber was painted with an aluminium paint to deaden the radar pulses and so, again, reduce the chance of detection. This boat was nicknamed 'The White Puma'.

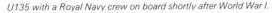

U135 with a Royal Navy crew on board shortly after World War I.

APPENDIX G: Armament in Royal Navy submarines

The submarine was the only naval vessel built to be armed effectively by one weapon—the torpedo. Twenty-eight years prior to the first Royal Navy submarine, the torpedo boat was designed and built in large numbers to carry the weapon but it has been more successfully employed by the submarine than by any surface vessel.

The torpedo in the Holland Class was 14 in calibre; in the A Class it was increased to 18 in and the D Class of 1908 first carried the 21 in torpedo. This is still the calibre used in nuclear powered submarines. Torpedoes, like all other forms of armament, have undergone considerable development over the years. The Tigerfish wire-guided torpedo was introduced in 1980 and was first used in anger against the Argentine cruiser *General Belgrano* on 2 May 1982. The type 7525, known as Spearfish, is a further improvement on the heavy 21 in torpedo and was announced in April 1982.

For surface use, the deck gun of the submarine varied from a single 3 pdr to a single 12 in, as fitted in the M Class. The most common deck gun for the submarine was the short 4 in mounted forward of the conning tower. This had a nominal muzzle velocity of 2,500 ft/sec and a range of four nm. In later years submarines were equipped with a number of weapons to combat aircraft, ranging from the .303 Lewis gun to the 20 mm Oerlikon, used by every ship in the Fleet. The 40 mm Bofors gun does not appear to have been part of a submarine armament. The 3 in HA/DP weapon, nominally the 12 pdr (sometimes 14 pdr) was also intended to be an anti-aircraft weapon. Their minimal directional equipment for high-level fire made their effectiveness questionable against aircraft.

More recently the missile with a guidance system has been proposed, and the Slam/Blow Pipe two-stage solid-fuel rocket with optical or radio guidance and an HE warhead have been on trial.

Polaris was the first intermediate-range ballistic missile (IRBM) developed for launching from a submerged submarine.

Type A1 was first fired successfully from USN S/M *George Washington* on 20 July 1960. It was subsequently developed to Type A3 which is powered by a two-stage solid propellant rocket motor. It has a built-in inertial guidance system which is motivated by geo-ballistic and navigational computers on board the launching submarine. These feed information to the IRBM system until the moment of launch after which it becomes entirely independent.

The missiles are mounted vertically in the submarine. The initial stage of launch is from steam pressure generated in the launch tube by firing a small rocket motor into a water chamber beneath it. After emergence at the surface the missile's own first stage is fired.

The missile is $32\frac{1}{4}$ ft long and $4\frac{1}{2}$ ft in diameter; the launch weight is 35,000 lbs and the range 2,800 nm. It is armed with the Chevaline system of independently targetted warheads.

The Trident system has been designated the successor to Polaris. This intercontinental ballistic missile (ICBM) carries eight independently targetted warheads. Sixteeen missiles are to be mounted in each submarine, giving a total of 128 target options. The warhead on each is to be about 100 kilotons. Trident is to be 34 ft long and 6 ft 2 in diameter; the launch weight is approx. 36,000 lbs and the missile has a range of 4,350 nm.

Harpoon is a tactical missile system with an effective range of 55–120 nm for surface to surface (SSM) or underwater to surface (USM) use. In this configuration the weapon is fired from a torpedo tube conventionally by compressed air, after which it utilises its built-in turbojet and rocket motors. Guidance is radar-programmed. Harpoon is 15 ft long, weights 1,470 lbs and has a speed of Mach 0.9. It carries a 500 lb HE or thermonuclear warhead and was test launched from HM S/M *Churchill* in April 1980.

A Spearfish 21 in torpedo.

A Tigerfish 21 in wire guided torpedo. The photograph clearly shows
the wire coil in its guard behind the contra-rotating propellers.

A Tigerfish 21 in torpedo being taken on board HM S/M Conqueror.

APPENDIX H: Submarine builders in the United Kingdom, Canada and the USA

Sir W. G. Armstrong Whitworth & Co Ltd, Newcastle upon Tyne, Northumberland

William Beardmore & Co Ltd, Dalmuir, Glasgow

Bethlehem Shipbuilding Corporation Ltd, Bethlehem, Pa, USA also at Fore River Plant, Quincy, Mass, USA, and Union Iron Works, San Francisco, USA

John Brown & Co Ltd, Clydebank

Cammell Laird & Co Ltd, Birkenhead

Canadian Vickers, Montreal, Canada

William Denny & Brothers, Dumbarton, Strathclyde, Scotland

HM Dockyard, Chatham, Kent

HM Dockyard, Devonport, Devon

HM Dockyard, Pembroke, Dyfed, Wales

HM Dockyard, Portsmouth, Hampshire

Fairfield Shipbuilding & Engineering Co Ltd, Govan, Glasgow

Palmers Shipbuilding & Iron Co, Hebburn, Tyne and Wear

Scotts Shipbuilding & Engineering Co Ltd, Greenock, Strathclyde, Scotland

Swan Hunter & Wigham Richardson Ltd, Wallsend, Tyne and Wear

J. I. Thornycroft & Co Ltd, Woolston, Hampshire

Vickers Ltd, Barrow-in-Furness, Cumbria

J. Samuel White & Co Ltd, Cowes, Isle of Wight

Yarrow & Co, Scotstoun, Strathclyde, Scotland

BIBLIOGRAPHY

The War at Sea, Captain S. W. Roskill, HMSO

Japanese Warships of World War II, A. J. Watts, Ian Allan

Warships or World War 1, H. M. Le Fleming, Ian Allan

Jane's Fighting Ships (various editions) Sampson Low & Marston

Jane's Pocket Book No 8, John E. Moore, Macdonald & Jane's

Warships of World War II, H. T. Lenton & J. J. Colledge, Ian Allan

Transactions of the Royal Institution of Naval Architects (various years), RINA, London

Axis Submarines, A. J. Watts, Macdonald & Jane's

Allied Submarines, A. J. Watts, Macdonald & Jane's

Jane's Pocket Book No 9, Denis Archer, Macdonald & Jane's

British Warships 1914–1919, F. J. Dittmar & J. J. Colledge, Ian Allan

Yard Shipbuilding List, Vickers Shipbuilding Group

German Warships of World War II, J. C. Taylor, Ian Allan

Warships of the Royal Navy, Captain J. E. Moore, RN, Macdonald & Jane's

British Escort Ships, H. T. Lenton, Macdonald & Jane's

The Development of H.M. Submarines from Holland No 1 (1901) to Porpoise (1930), A. N. Harrison, Ministry of Defence.

HMS Forth, a submarine depot ship in Devonport dockyard, 1962.

INDEX